CHAPTERS IN CARIBBEAN HISTORY 1

EDITORS

DOUGLAS HALL
Professor of History, University of the West Indies
ELSA GOVEIA
Professor of West Indian History, University of the West Indies
F. ROY AUGIER
Senior Lecturer in History, University of the West Indies

The Development of the Plantations to 1750

An era of West Indian prosperity 1750-1775

RICHARD SHERIDAN MA PhD

Professor of Economic History
University of Kansas

 Caribbean Universities Press

Caribbean Universities Press   Barbados
Outside the Caribbean
c/o Ginn & Company Ltd
18 Bedford Row   London W C 1   England
© University of the West Indies
Department of History 1970
First published 1970
SBN 602 21567 6
017007
Printed in England by
Willmer Brothers Limited   Birkenhead

Contents

The Development of the Plantations to 1750   *page* 7

An Era of West Indian Prosperity 1750–1775   71

Editorial Note

We are engaged in the writing and editing of a History of the Caribbean and we are grateful for financial assistance received from the Ford Foundation.

We hope to achieve a regional approach, as far as the diverse histories of the various territories permit, and we believe that the work can greatly stimulate research and teaching throughout the area.

Rather than hold contributions until the entire History has been assembled, we have decided to publish accepted contributions in this series as they appear, and many of the Chapters will be contributed by scholars abroad. At the end of the book, following the index, will be found a draft outline of the contents of the History.

In this first number of the Series, we include two Chapters by Richard Sheridan, Professor of Economic History at the University of Kansas.

D. G. HALL

E. V. GOVEIA

F. R. AUGIER

University of the West Indies
Mona

The Development of the
Plantations to 1750

The Development of the Plantations to 1750

After more than three centuries of European penetration into out-lying parts of the globe, the dominant theme of recent history has been the revolt of three-quarters of the world against colonialism and the emergence of new nations to seek their place in the sun. Moreover, overseas lands which have long since thrown off the yoke of colonialism have been the scene of social unrest, as witness the Negro revolts in the United States. If one seeks for elements common to these nations and peoples, it will be seen that, apart from their former colonial status, the greater portion of these regions lies in tropical and subtropical latitudes inhabited by Africans and Asiatics.

By means of mines and plantations, land and forced labour were linked to European capital and management to produce precious metals, foodstuffs, and raw materials to supply the expanding markets of Europe and North America. From the vantage point of the colonial revolt it will be instructive to re-examine the role of tropical colonies, and particularly the West Indian plantation colonies, in the century or more leading up to the democratic and industrial revolutions.

I

Variously described as 'treasure islands' or 'precious gems in the crown of trade', plantation colonies were widely regarded in the age of mercantilism as valuable adjuncts to European nations. First and foremost, they supplied Europeans with commodities that could not be grown in the cold climates of the north. To such foodstuffs and beverages as sugar, rice, tea, coffee, cocoa, and rum, were added the weed *Nicotiana tabacum* and a wide variety of dyes, drugs, vegetable fibres, and rare woods. Private vices became public virtues as new cravings led Europeans to expand their output of manufactures to exchange for tropical wares. Manufacturing, shipping, trade, finance, and exchequer revenues thus expanded in response to the demand for exotics. As Sir Josiah Child expressed it, 'Profit and Power ought joyntly to be considered';[1] profit to the rising mercantile class, power to the nation state.

Numerous writers emphasised the role of tropical plantation colonies in the expansion of European nations, Louis XIV wrote to the Governor of Martinique in 1670: 'The more the colonies differ from the mother country in products, so much more nearly are they perfect, as in the case of the Antilles'.[2] About a century later Arthur Young, the English agricultural writer, observed:

> The great benefit resulting from colonies is the cultivation of staple commodities different from those of the mother-country; that, instead of being obliged to purchase them of foreigners at the expense possibly of treasure, they may be had from settlements in exchange for manufactures.[3]

While it was Young's opinion that the North American colonies produced only trifling staples, 'those to the south, on the contrary, are immensely valuable—indeed of such infinite importance to this nation, that *general expressions* of the benefit of our settlements should never be indulged'.[4]

The antecedents of the plantation colonies can be traced to the sixteenth century when the centre of European power began to shift from the Iberian countries to Holland, France and England. Included among the notable events of this century were the rise of the Dutch Republic, the defeat of the Spanish Armada, daring privateering raids into Caribbean waters, and the first attempts to establish colonies of settlement in North America and Guiana. Caribbean islands were regarded as strategic bases from which to attack the Spanish colonies. However, altered circumstances might make it feasible to convert such bases into colonies producing agricultural staples for European markets.

Such altered circumstances, chiefly of an economic and social

---

[1] Sir Josiah Child, *A Discourse about Trade* (London, 1690), p. 93.
[2] Quoted in José L. Suárez, *Carácter de la Revólucion Americana* (Buenos Aires, 1917), pp. 6–7.
[3] Arthur Young, *Political Essays Concerning the Present State of the British Empire* (London, 1772), p. 274.
[4] *Ibid.*, pp. 326–7.

nature, were forthcoming in the early decades of the seventeenth century. Spain's hold on the New World, which had weakened in the late decades of the sixteenth century, was undermined after 1600 when imports of American treasure fell precipitately. The merchants of Northern Europe, who had benefited indirectly from the treasure flowing into Spain, thus faced a shrinkage in their profits and trade. Moreover, the outbreak of the Thirty Years' War in 1618 contributed to the collapse of the Baltic trade. Several years later French merchants suffered heavy losses in the Levant trade. The economic slump in England was complicated by a demographic crisis stemming from poor harvests, enclosures, and the conversion of arable fields into pasture for sheep grazing.

In this setting, merchants who had looked to the Continent for markets and sources of supply began to shift their theatre of operations to overseas trade, while the projectors of colonies gained popular support with promises to reduce social tension at home by providing an outlet for surplus population.

The opportunity for widespread colonisation in the West Indies came after 1623 when the northern powers resumed hostilities against Spain and Portugal. In the following year the Dutch West India Company began the conquest of northern Brazil at a time when Portugal was a province of Spain. While the efforts of Spain were diverted to the defence of Brazil, the northern nations began to seize on the islands of the Lesser Antilles. In the words of Professor Newton, 'After 1625 swarms of English and French colonists poured like flies upon the rotting carcass of Spain's empire in the Caribbean, and within ten years the West Indian scene was changed for ever'.[5]

Life was generally nasty, brutish and short for the pioneer settlers in the Caribbean. 'Ships were sent with men, provisions, and working tools, to cut down the Woods, and clear the ground, so they might plant provisions to keep them alive', wrote Richard Ligon, the seventeenth century planter-historian of Barbados. Having cleared a piece of ground, 'they planted Potatoes, Plantins, and Mayes, with some other fruits; which, with the Hogflesh they found, serv'd only to keep life and soul together'.[6]

---

[5] A. P. Newton, *The European Nations in the West Indies 1493–1688* (London, 1933), pp. 149–50.
[6] Richard Ligon, *A True and Exact History of the Island of Barbados* (London, 1673), p. 24.

After a short period of uneasy friendship with the settlers, the Carib Indians were exterminated, forced into bondage, or confined to certain islands in the Lesser Antilles. Besides having to repulse hostile Indians, the French and English settlers in St Christopher were attacked by a fleet of Spanish galleons and armed merchantmen in 1629.

But the European came to the New World to improve his material well-being by securing land that was unencumbered by ancient custom and law. He grew subsistence crops while he searched for staples that would enable him to partake of the luxuries of Europe. During their first year in St Christopher the English settlers built a fort, planted provisions, and made a crop of tobacco. Frenchmen on the same island were encouraged to grow tobacco by a Dutch captain who arrived in 1628. Lacking substantial means of their own and being poorly supplied with trade credit, the first generation of settlers occupied small farms and combined subsistence and cash crops—chiefly tobacco, cotton, indigo, cocao, and ginger. Then came the sugar revolution of the 1640s and 1650s, first in Barbados and later extending to other settlements in the West Indies.

II

Viewed from the perspective of post-Roman European history, 'the plantation was an absolutely unprecedented social, economic, and political institution, and by no means simply an innovation in the organizations of agriculture', writes Professor Mintz.[7] Numerous cultures streamed into the Caribbean island world from Asia, Africa, Europe, South America and North America, bringing together economic plants, hoe cultivators, managers, capital, technology, livestock, foodstuffs and building materials. These elements were combined in varying proportions with tropical soils and climate to minimise the costs of production, marketing, defence, and labour discipline. As these cultural influences were more or less common to all West Indian plantation colonies, they will be considered briefly before turning to comparative studies on an island, mainland, and plantation basis.

[7]Sidney W. Mintz, Foreword to Ramiro Guerra y Sanchez, *Sugar and Society in the Caribbean: An Economic History of Cuban Agriculture* (New Haven, 1964), p. xiv.

The extension of agriculture into the tropical zone of the New World was contingent upon the appropriation and development of energy sources. Since man is both a producer and consumer of energy, one way of looking at history is to view it as a process by which man has used his own energy output to master and utilise other forms of energy. He has made use of various types of converters to transform energy from one form to another, ever striving to devise more technically efficient converters which increase the ratio between useful output and total input. Before the age of steam power, man depended chiefly on animate sources of energy—his own labour and that of domesticated plants and animals. He also made some progress in devising converters to harness inanimate sources of power, as in the development of sailing vessels, wind mills and water wheels. Sugar plantations combined animate and inanimate converters in an agro-industrial economy that may well be described as power-intensive. The animate converters consisted of Negro slaves and domesticated plants and animals, while the inanimate converters took the form of wind mills, water mills, and tide mills.

It was of particular significance that most of these converters were imported from abroad, that their replacement rate was generally high, and that they were brought to the plantations in another type of converter, the sailing ship. Accessibility to factor inputs and markets depended upon the ocean and the sailing ship which the Portuguese had developed in order to venture into unknown waters. Moreover, the ship played an important part in determining the location of plantation colonies, for its movement was determined by winds and currents which made some areas more accessible than others. Compared with Brazil, the first plantation colony of note, the Caribbean was not only closer to northwestern Europe but relatively quick and easy passages to and from the islands were made possible by the northeast trade winds, the Gulf Stream, and westerly winds. Proximity to the temperate zone colonies in North America was another advantage which the West Indians held over the Brazilians.

Considerations of defence and transport initially favoured small islands over other areas of possible plantation development. Since ships 'ran' downwind but had to beat their way upwind, islands to windward were more easily defended than those to leeward. Moreover, the high ratio of coastline to land area facilitated water-borne traffic. Early maps of the sugar islands show how sea transport influenced the location of economic activity. Plantations were most numerous on the leeward side because they depended on the services provided by the chief ports. The ports, in turn, were situated on bays which provided shelter and easy departure for ships. As plantation culture spread on a given island, coastal sites were preferred to interior sites. Plantations were generally long and narrow, the narrow side fronting on the sea. 'The reason for this', as Professor Pares points out, 'was that from the first foundation of the colonies all settlers had to enjoy an equal chance at sea-transportation for their produce, which was the only kind of transportation then in existence'.[8]

Ships brought the first colonists who were supplied with foodstuffs, tools, livestock, and other accoutrements of European civilisation. Numerous difficulties were experienced in adapting European agriculture to a tropical environment. In fact, most of the settlements went through a 'starving time' before a foothold was established. From the colonists' standpoint it was fortunate that, for a time at least, the Amerindians were inclined to be friendly. During this uneasy interval the European learned the strange arts of tropical agriculure from the Arawak and Carib.

Writing in 1682, an Englishman called attention to the 'many fruits, plants, and vegetables, which through the advantages of commerce and navigation, all the countries of Europe now enjoy, though unknown to older times'.[9] European consumption habits were greatly influenced by these fruits, plants and vegetables, of which some were obtained directly from indigenous peoples by means of barter, while others were transported from one continent to another to be grown on plantations. Root crops, the chief food of the Arawaks and Caribs, consisted of manioc, sweet potatoes, yams, arrowroot, and other edible tubers and fleshy roots. To these were added seed crops such as maize, beans, peas, pumpkins and squashes. Indigenous plants which came to play an important role in international trade were tobacco, cotton, cocoa, indigo, and a variety of drugs, dyes and rare woods.

By means of commerce and navigation, plants were carried both

---

[8] Richard Pares, 'Merchants and Planters', *Economic History Review*, Supplement 4 (Cambridge, 1960), pp. 9, 61–2, n. 46.

[9] Adam Anderson, *Historical and Chronological Deduction of the Origin of Commerce* (6 vols. Dublin, 1790), Vol. III, p. 104.

ways across vast oceans to be adapted to new habitats. Tobacco, potatoes, maize, and cocoa, among other plants, were carried to Europe, Africa, and Asia, while in the reverse direction moved rice, sugar-cane, coffee and citrus. Rice was carried from Madagascar to South Carolina about 1693 to become a leading staple. Coffee, which is thought to have originated in Abyssinia, was of commercial importance in Arabia for several centuries. The Dutch carried it from Arabia to Java in 1699 and Surinam in 1714. From here it was introduced into Martinique, Guadeloupe, and Jamaica in the decade of the 1720s.

The vegetative selection and reproduction of the wild sugar-cane is thought to have developed in southeast Asia in Neolithic times. From this centre of what Professor Sauer calls the 'old planter culture', the sugar-cane was dispersed to other areas, chiefly to the Middle East and Mediterranean before its migration to the New World.[10] Successive civilisations carried the sugar-cane ever westward, the Moslems eventually planting it on several Mediterranean islands, the Barbary Coast, and Southern Spain.

As islands played a part in the transit of the Mediterranean, so the sugar-cane reached the New World by means of island stepping stones. It was from the Canary Islands, where Spaniards had introduced the plant about 1480, that Columbus on his second voyage obtained sugar-canes, experienced cultivators, livestock, 'the pips and seeds of oranges, lemons and citrons, melons and every kind of vegetable' to carry to Hispaniola. In 1425, Prince Henry the Navigator directed the sugar-cane to be carried from Sicily to the Madeira Islands, from whence it was introduced into Brazil about 1515. From Hispaniola, Brazil, and the coastal region of the Guianas the cane was introduced into the Lesser Antilles.

Just as the people of the Netherlands brought the commercial civilisation of the Mediterranean and Iberian countries to Northern Europe, so it was that Dutchmen and Portuguese Jews transferred the centre of the sugar industry from Brazil to the West Indies. Professor Canabrava has traced this northward migration in three stages. 'The first expansion was accomplished by the Dutch merchants, with purely mercantile motives. This occurred during the period of the Dutch domination of Brazil between the years 1636–1650 and especially during 1647–1650, having as a centre of focus the Eng-

[10] Carl O. Sauer, *Agricultural Origins and Dispersals* (New York, 1952), pp. 20–22.

lish island of Barbados'. The next stage began in 1654 with the expulsion of the Dutch and Portuguese Jews from Brazil. Those who migrated to the West Indies went chiefly to the French islands of Guadeloupe and Martinique, where they divulged the techniques that they knew, supplied capital and slaves on long-term credit, and linked the new centres of sugar production to European markets. Lastly, there was the re-emigration of Dutchmen and Jews to the Greater Antilles, as for example the movement from Barbados and Surinam to Jamaica, or from Martinique to St Domingue.[11]

Technology was one aspect of the Dutch-Judaic contribution which deserves special mention. Having produced the sweetening substance for more than a century before 1650, the Portuguese and Sephardic Jews developed the art of sugar manufacture to a high state. These skills were transmitted to Dutchmen during the occupation of Brazil, after which the Dutch and Sephardic Jews carried the sugar mill technology to the West Indies.

The most expensive piece of mechanical equipment on a sugar plantation was the mill for crushing the canes. Millstones were commonly used in the Old World sugar industry until 1449, when Pietro Speciale, Prefect of Sicily, invented the roller mill. It consisted of three rollers of wood (or wood encased with iron) which stood upright and turned on pivots. 'The middlemost roller', wrote a contemporary, 'is moved by the wind, water or by cattle; by the same kind of mechanism as the corn and other mills in Europe: the two others are turned by this, each of the three having for that purpose a cog and teeth at the upper end'.[12]

The first mills to be constructed in Hispaniola and Brazil depended on the living power of horses, oxen or slaves. Besides their limited cane crushing capacity, cattle mills took a heavy toll of livestock during the harvest season when there were extraordinary demands for cart horses and oxen.

Planters thus turned to more economical forms of power wherever environmental conditions permitted. Rivers, topography, and wind currents determined the selection of water mills, wind mills, and tide mills. Islands and continental coastal plains varied widely in

[11] A. P. Canabrava, 'A Influência do Brasil na têcnica do fabrico de açucar nas Antilhas francesas e inglesas no meado do século XVII', *Anuário da Faculdade de Ciências Econômicas e Administrativas, 1946–47* (Sao Paulo, 1947), p. 76.
[12] Anon., *The Art of Making Sugar* (London, 1752), p. 10.

resource endowments. Small islands in the Lesser Antilles, particularly Barbados and Antigua, had inadequate rivers to generate water power but they were well suited to wind mills owing to relatively level topography and unimpeded trade winds. More varied conditions were found in the islands of Martinique, Guadeloupe, St Domingue and Jamaica. Mountain ranges might so impede the trade winds that wind mills were only feasible on the windward side. Yet by disturbing the moisture-laden atmosphere, mountains contributed to increased precipitation and stream flow and thus made it advantageous to construct dams, canals, and aqueducts to divert water to sugar mills on the plains. If sufficiently abundant, water might be diverted to irrigate areas of inadequate rainfall on the leeward side of the mountains. Other areas were suited to tide mills. On the coastal plains of the Guianas, water was stored in canals during the spring-tide and then released at low water to power the mills.[13]

In deciding upon the optimum size of his plantation, the proprietor had to consider such factors as milling capacity, the economies of large-scale production, and land transport. Larger and more efficient mills generally meant larger cane acreage and labour force. One contemporary said that a water mill processed between forty and fifty cart loads of canes in a 24-hour period, as compared with twenty-five to thirty-five cartloads for a cattle mill. Moreover, plantation size was influenced by economies of scale. Edward Long, the Jamaica planter-historian, said that 'the same Buildings and many incidental charges are much the same for an Estate that makes 50 or 60 hogsheads of Sugar yearly as one that makes 100, so that little more is wanting than a greater strength of Negroes and Cattle, in proportion to the Quantity'.[14]

Other factors set limits to plantation size. Owing to rapid fermentation, newly-cut canes had to be milled within about 24 hours if sugar of marketable quality was to be produced. Milling time was thus limited, while, on the other hand, transport from the field to the mill was slow and cumbersome, consisting of pack animals, cattle carts, and slaves carrying the canes on their heads. For these and

[13] For a description of a tide mill see John Stedman, *Expedition to Surinam ... from the years 1772 to 1777*, ed. Christopher Bryant (London, 1963), pp. 120–21.
[14] Edward Long, *The History of Jamaica* (3 vols. London, 1774), Vol. I, p. 448.

other reasons Professor Pares maintains that 'however well the sugar work was sited, it could not profitably serve an estate of more than 300/350 negroes, tending an acreage of sugar cane which probably would not exceed 300 in all'.[15]

Water mills and wind mills replaced cattle mills on many plantations, but not where inanimate power sources were lacking. Numerous plantations thus continued to depend on horse power. Moreover, the movement toward monoculture witnessed a growing demand for draft animals and manure. Livestock husbandry proved quite successful in the large islands, though much less so in small islands where cane lands encroached upon pastures and fodder crops. As local needs outpaced domestic breeding capacity, livestock was imported from abroad in growing numbers. Europe was the initial source of supply despite almost prohibitive shipping charges. In time, the livestock supply centre shifted to neighbouring colonies. Cattle, mules and horses were obtained from the Spanish colonies and the English settlements in North America. Proximity to the temperate-zone colonies yielded other benefits.

Supplies of North American foodstuffs, building materials, and livestock came to the English sugar islands during the Civil Wars. By the Restoration period several mercantile writers had begun to warn the government of the consequences of growing intercolonial trade. But the trade continued to grow; it did so to such an extent that after the Treaty of Utrecht (1713), the North Americans were able to supply cheap intermediate goods to both the British and foreign sugar colonies. Relationships between temperate and tropical colonies were mutually beneficial. While sugar specialisation in the Caribbean was an incentive to the development of settlement colonies to the north, similar settlement projects in Brazil failed completely.[16]

'Sugar is made by man and power', writes Professor Ortiz.[17] We have seen how man used his own energy output to domesticate plants and animals and to utilise the energy of wind and falling water. But man has also mastered and utilised the power of other men. European settlers in the tropics have laboured independently, they have

[15] Pares, 'Merchants and Planters', pp. 24–5.
[16] Celso Furtado, *The Economic Growth of Brazil* (Berkeley and Los Angeles, 1963), pp. 60–6.
[17] Fernando Otiz, *Cuban Counterpoint: Tobacco and Sugar* (New York, 1947), p. 49.

drawn on the labour power of European bond servants, they have impressed indigenous peoples into slavery, and they have imported chattel slaves and contract labourers from other tropical countries.

Although there was no inherent physiological reason why Europeans could not be acclimatised to agricultural labour in the tropics, economic factors, as Dr Williams makes clear, limited the all-white labour régime chiefly to the pioneer stages of settlement and small staple culture.[18] At the outset of the sugar revolution, voluntary emigration to the West Indies had greatly diminished. Resort was increasingly had to white servants, a growing proportion of whom were prisoners-of-war, debtors, sturdy beggars, orphans and criminals. Profitable staple production, as Edward Gibbon Wakefield observed, required combined and constant labour.[19] Bond servants were not only difficult to supervise in group undertakings, but their labour services were of short duration. Having laboured from three to seven years, and thus legally discharged their obligations, newly-freed servants commonly left behind the scene of their hated bondage. Many became pioneers on new tropical frontiers.

The African contribution to Caribbean plantation society has not always been sufficiently appreciated. Rather than being primitive food gatherers and hunters, the Africans in the old slaving area had a culture which contained such elements as settled community life, political organisation, handicrafts, art and religion. Though differing in levels of culture, the tribal agrarian economies of West Africa had rudimentary forms of occupational specialisation, exchange, money, markets and metallurgy. On the other hand, Africans lacked firearms and ocean-going vessels which gave Europeans military supremacy and mobility in pursuit of the slave trade. The African was a hoe cultivator and not infrequently a skilled artisan before he was brought to the West Indies. The image of Africa as a reservoir of undifferentiated, crude labour power is patently false. Actually, Africans replaced Europeans in a variety of craft and supervisory occupations on plantations in the West Indies.

Neither should it be thought that the African was resigned to a system which appropriated his labour power without monetary compensation or the promise of freedom. Instead of fitting the stereo-

[18] Eric Williams, *Capitalism and Slavery* (Chapel Hill, 1944), pp. 19–29.
[19] Edward Gibbon Wakefield, *A View of the Art of Colonization* (Oxford, 1914), pp. 175–80.

type of the docile, tractable, happy servant, he was more often deeply resentful of his life of bondage, taking advantage of opportunities to escape to the wilds and even plotting mass uprising. It will be seen that insurrection and escape were more common in large islands and coastal areas than in small and densely populated islands.

Slave labour has been profitable in a business sense only under certain conditions:

(a) Where it has been possible to maintain slaves very cheaply;
(b) where there has been an opportunity for regular recruitment through a well-supplied slave market;
(c) in agricultural production on a large scale of the plantation type, or in very simple industrial processes.[20]

Even though the ability to satisfy these conditions varied in time and place, there are strong grounds for asserting that they were substantially met in the period of this study. Plantation units tended to increase in acreage, labour force, and capitalised value, thus permitting unskilled field hands to be joined to artisans and overseers in a system of occupational specialisation and division of labour. Slave maintenance costs, consisting chiefly of food, clothing, shelter, and medical attendance, were probably less in the West Indies than in Brazil. Foodstuffs were by far the largest item, but it will be seen that slaves provisioned themselves to a large extent in some of the colonies, and that relatively cheap foodstuffs and building materials were imported from North America.

Historians of slavery have often argued that even if humanitarian sentiments were lacking, planters were led by motives of self-interest to ensure the health, well-being, and longevity of their slaves. While it is true that individual plantation documents often support this contention, overwhelming evidence to the contrary is available in the form of slave trade and population statistics which show that the labour force was *not* self-renewing. From the calculations of fifteen English and French 'authors of credit', William Dickson concluded that 'the labouring lives of *bought* Field-slaves exceed not seven years in the gross', while 'the Slaves collectively, *bought* and *bred*, die off and are renewed, in about *fifteen* years'. He estimated that

---

[20] Max Weber, *The Theory of Social and Economic Organization*, tr. A. R. Henderson and Talcott Parsons, (London, 1947), pp. 253-4.

slaves in the West Indies died off at a rate of more than twice as fast as the rest of the human race.[21] Among the reasons for this high mortality were the high ratio of males to females which led to promiscuous breeding habits, inadequate care of infants, disease, accidents, hard labour, and a low-protein diet. 'Above all, however, the slave population must have been kept down by under-feeding and overworking', writes Professor Pares.[22]

Planters thus turned to the labour reservoir in Africa. It has been conservatively estimated that in the course of four centuries Africa supplied the plantations and mines of the New World with 15 million slaves: nearly 900,000 in the sixteenth century, nearly 3 million in the seventeenth century, 7 million in the eighteenth century, and 4 million in the nineteenth century.[23] Immigrants from Africa probably exceeded those from Europe until the early years of the nineteenth century.

However impressive these global figures may be, the individual planter was concerned with the profitability of slavery, that is, the return above first cost and maintenance charges, together with appropriate interest rate adjustments, figured over the working life of his slaves. When he compared the cost of rearing slaves and paying the purchase price of newly-imported slaves, he generally found it cheaper to buy than to breed. Since Africa bore the cost of rearing and then lost a considerable portion of her young adults to the New World, it might be thought that the labour reservoir would be depleted seriously. Certain coastal areas were depopulated, it is true, but there is little reason to doubt the considered opinion of Dr Malthus that, despite emigration, wars and vice, the population of Africa was 'constantly pressing against the means of subsistence'.[24]

III

The tendency for African slaves and other energy converters to be concentrated in the West India islands is suggested by the statistics of sugar production in Tables I and II.

[21] William Dickson, *Mitigation of Slavery* (London, 1814), pp. 453–7.
[22] Pares, 'Merchants and Planters', pp. 38–9.
[23] Robert R. Kucynski, *Population Movements* (Oxford, 1936), pp 6–17.
[24] Thomas R. Malthus, *An Essay on Population* (2 vols. London, 1958), Vol. I, p. 91.

Table I

Sugar production in the American
Tropical Colonies, 1741–5 and 1766–70[1]
(Annual Averages in Tons)

	1741–5	*1766–70*
French	64,675[2]	77,923[2]
British	41,043	74,452
Portuguese	34,000[3]	20,400[4]
Danish	730[5]	8,230[6]
Dutch	9,210[7]	6,800[8]
Spanish	2,000	5,200[9]
Total	151,658	193,005

NOTES: (1) The quantities shown in Tables I and II are the legal imports into the metropolitan countries. Colonies which exported less than 1,000 tons annually are omitted. (2) See Table II, notes 1, 2, 3, 6, 7 (3) 1760 (4) 1776 (5) 1755 (6) 1770 (7) 1740, 1745 (8) 1765, 1770 (9) 1764–8

SOURCE: Noel Deerr, *History of Sugar* (1949), Vol. I, pp. 112, 131, 193–8, 235–6, 245; John Campbell, *Considerations on the Nature of the Sugar Trade* (1763), p. 54; David MacPherson, *Annals of Commerce* (1805), Vol. III, p. 262; R. M. N. Panday, *Agriculture in Surinam 1650–1950* (1959), p. 19; Jacobo de la Pezuela, *Diccionario . . . de la Isla de Cuba* (1863), Vol. I, p. 62

Table I shows that only the two mainland colonies of Brazil (Portuguese) and Surinam (Dutch) exported 1,000 tons or more annually in the period of this study. In the aggregate, these mainland colonies accounted for 28.5 per cent and 14.1 per cent in 1741–5 and 1766–70 respectively, compared with 71.5 and 85.9 for the Caribbean islands.

It is also evident from Table I that of the six European nations possessing sugar colonies in the New World, France and Great Britain were the pre-eminent powers in the mid-eighteenth century period. The French colonies accounted for 42.6 per cent and 40.4 per cent of the production in 1741–5 and 1766–70 respectively, compared with 27.1 and 38.6 for the British. The remaining 30.3 and 21.0 were distributed among the colonies of Portugal, Denmark, Holland, and Spain. Brazil's share declined from 22.4 to 10.6.

When it is considered that sugar was produced on at least twenty-one islands in the Caribbean Sea, it is remarkable that five islands accounted for three-fifths of total American production, and that ten islands contributed between two-thirds and four-fifths of the total. Of the four islands in the Greater Antilles—Cuba, Hispaniola, Puerto Rico, and Jamaica, the two colonies of St Domingue and Jamaica accounted for 56.2 per cent in 1741–5 and 53.8 per cent in 1766–70. Cuba, which is almost as large as all of the other West Indian islands put together, was a late starter in the sugar industry, accounting for only 3.2 per cent of the total in 1766–70. Even further behind was Puerto Rico, where only 1,222 tons of sugar were produced in 1776. On the other hand, some eighteen islands in the Lesser Antilles produced approximately one-third of the New World sugar in the mid-eighteenth century period. That most of these islands were marginal producers is revealed by the fact that the seven islands shown in Table II (Antigua, St Christopher, Martinique, St Croix, Guadeloupe, Barbados, and Grenada) accounted for approximately ninety per cent of the total of the Lesser Antilles. Altogether, these seven islands comprised only 2.5 per cent of the land area of the ten leading sugar island colonies.

Table II

Sugar Production of the Ten Leading Caribbean
Islands, 1741–5 and 1766–70
(Annual Averages in Tons)

	Area in Square Miles	1741–5	1766–70
St Domingue (French)	10,714	42,400[1]	61,247[2]
Jamaica (British)	4,411	15,578	36,021
Antigua (British)	108	6,229	10,690
St Christopher (British)	68	7,299	9,701
Martinique (French)	425	14,163[3]	8,778
St Croix (Danish)	84	730[4]	8,230[5]
Guadeloupe (French)	583	8,112[6]	7,898[7]
Barbados (British)	166	6,640	7,819
Grenada (British)	120	——	6,552
Cuba (Spanish)	44,164	2,000	5,200[8]
Total	60,843	103,151	162,136

NOTES: (1) 1742 (2) 1767, 1768 (3) 1741, 1744, 1745 (4) 1755 (5) 1770
(6) 1730, 1761 (7) 1767 (8) 1764–68
SOURCE: Same as in Table I.

Since the production figures in Tables I and II raise more questions than can be answered in the brief compass of this study, it will be necessary to focus on some of the major comparisons. Certainly the two major colonial powers—France and England—deserve special recognition in view of their involvement in plantation society. Comparison and contrast between the developments in smaller and larger islands, between small and great planters and estates, and the internal organisation of plantations are other important topics. As the previous section has dealt with common elements in plantation society, we may now turn to the chief differences in the colonial systems of France and England.

The truly developed mercantile system called for intercontinental and insular specialisation and division of labour, of a metropolis and its colonies linked together by exclusive trade. Not only should there be a reciprocal flow of temperate and tropical goods between the metropolis and the plantations, but also a flow of crude foodstuffs and raw materials between the plantations and the colonies of settlement. Moreover, the metropolis should use its military and economic power to ensure the flow of slaves to the plantations. In a system of imperial interdependency, no one region should develop more rapidly than the others. Thus, the ideal situation was balanced growth in the temperate and tropical regions of the Empire.

Though practice diverged widely from theory, England came closer to achieving these goals than her chief rival, France. In the course of the seventeenth century England's Atlantic Empire assumed its characteristic features. Puritan and Quaker settlements became supply centres for the plantations. Colonies specialising in tobacco, rice, sugar and other staples developed in subtropical regions extending from Maryland to Barbados. Access to the labour reservoir in Africa came after victory in the Anglo-Dutch wars. And, finally, the navigation acts of the Commonwealth and Restoration governments went far to integrate these elements into a viable mercantile empire.

Distracted by continental wars and lacking a vigorous commercial class, France lagged behind England in developing her West Indian plantations despite the heroic efforts of Colbert. According to Professor Hauser, it was the fever of speculation unleashed by John Law's 'System' which gave new life to overseas commerce and to industry. 'This trade was carried on to a large extent with the French

24

colonial empire, which, although it had been grievously curtailed in 1763, still preserved in St Domingo, "the pearl of the Antilles".[25] Even before the curtailment of her empire in North America, France had begun to concentrate her limited resources on her sugar colonies. In accounting for the rapid expansion of the French West Indies, contemporary observers pointed to relaxation of trade restrictions, lower taxes, government support of the African trade, sober and industrious colonists, humane treatment of slaves, and fertile and well-watered lands.

Notwithstanding these advantages, or alleged advantages, the French plantations developed in the face of formidable handicaps. Unlike England, France failed to establish tobacco, rice, and indigo colonies on the mainland; her 'sugar' colonies in consequence supplied a wider variety of tropical staples than their British counterparts. Moreover, France lacked temperate-zone colonies capable of supplying quantities of fish, flour, building materials, containers and horses. Although illicit trade with the English and Spanish colonies overcame this handicap to some extent, French planters probably devoted more land to provision culture and livestock grazing than their English rivals. Since the wars of the eighteenth century affected the French colonies much more than the British, a régime of self-sufficiency was frequently necessary if French planters and their slaves were to avoid starvation. Inferior seapower probably influenced the French to concentrate sugar production on their most easily defended islands. At the same time numerous islands in the Lesser Antilles were settled to supply the sugar islands with ground provisions, livestock, and building materials, as well as to grow minor staples for the European market. Moreover, the extent to which British merchants supplied slaves to the French planters is indicative of French inferiority in this department. Thus, it would appear that the more rapid expansion of the French planatations must be explained on grounds other than the cost of imported factors of production.

[25] Henri Hauser, 'The Characteristic Features of French Economic History from the Middle of the 16th to the Middle of the 18th Century', *The Economic History Review*, Vol IV, no. 3 (October, 1933), pp. 268–9.

IV

To illustrate the similarities and differences that existed between the French and British colonies and to compare and contrast the developments in the smaller and larger islands, four plantation colonies have been singled out for brief treatment. In the Lesser Antilles, the British island of Barbados will be compared with the French island of Martinique, while in the Greater Antilles, the British island of Jamaica will be compared with the French colony of St Domingue.* Both of the smaller islands were for many years the leading sugar colonies of their respective metropolises. However, during the second quarter of the eighteeenth century they were overtaken by their sister colonies in the Greater Antilles.

Barbados was first settled in 1627 by a group of Englishmen under the auspices of Sir William Courteen, a prominent merchant-adventurer of London. Finding the island uninhabited, he despatched a ship to Guiana where the captain 'furnished himselfe with rootes, plants, fowles, tobacco seeds, sugger canes and other matterialls, togither with thirty two Indians which he carried to the said Iland for the Planting thereof'.[26]

Having learned the rudiments of planting from the Indians, the settlers began to grow a variety of foodstuffs and cash crops, of which tobacco and cotton were most prominent. In the course of two decades Barbados became the most populous colony in the West Indies. In 1645, some 11,200 of the 18,300 effective men on the island were proprietors; much of the island at this time was divided into small farms ranging from five to thirty acres.

The Barbadian sugar industry dates from 1637 when a Dutchman came to the island and made sugar from canes he had introduced from Brazil. But the English Civil Wars broke out as soon as production had started, and Dutchmen began to abandon Brazil. It was in these circumstances of disrupted production in Brazil, high sugar prices in Europe, and limited commercial intercourse between England and her colonies that Dutch capital, credit, and plantership came to the aid of the Barbadians. But not all of the credit should be given to Dutchmen and Portuguese Jews. Beginning in 1650,

* Small and large island comparisons will be confined chiefly to Barbados and Jamaica.
[26] *Henry Powell's Examination*, Trinity College Dublin MSS. G. 14, 15.

several London merchants took an active part in fostering the sugar industry; at the same time they persuaded Cromwell to subdue the Royalist government of Barbados.

The chief characteristics of the sugar revolution were land consolidation, re-emigration of small proprietors and indentured servants, and the introduction of Negro slaves. Between 1645 and 1667, according to one observer, the number of proprietors declined from 11,200 to 745. As an example in point, one sugar plantation had been formerly occupied by forty proprietors. Having been 'wormed out of their small settlements by their more suttle and greedy neighbours', as many as 30,000 people left Barbados between 1650 and 1680.[27] Indentured servants met some of the growing labour requirements, but they were rapidly overtaken by Negro slaves. From an estimated fifty Africans in 1629, the slave population increased to about 6,000 in 1643, to 20,000 in 1655, and upwards of 30,000 in 1666. By 1667, according to John Scott, the making of sugar was 'managed Principally by Negro Slaves, who besides their purchase stood their Masters in little more than a Small Quantity of Land, to Plant Indian Corne, beanes, Potatoes, bonanoes, Plantans, Yams, &c. The Provisions of the Cuntry . . .'[28]

Barbados enjoyed its most prosperous period in the 1650s and 1660s. Its property value, according to one contemporary, increased seventeen-fold between 1643 and 1666; in the latter year their 'plate, jewels, and household stuff were estimated at £500,000, their buildings very fair and beautiful, and their houses like castles, their sugar houses and Negroes' huts show themselves from the sea like so many small towns, each defended by its castle'.[29]

After the revolutionary changes of the early decades of the sugar industry, consolidation proceeded more slowly and planters were concerned to add slaves and equipment and to improve the efficiency of their estates. The islanders became increasingly dependent on imported supplies as more and more resources were devoted to sugar production. So great was this dependence by 1672 that Governor

---

[27] Alfred D. Chandler, 'The Expansion of Barbados', *The Journal of the Barbados Museum and Historical Society*, Vol. XIII (May and November, 1946), pp. 106–14.

[28] John Scott, *The Description of Barbados*, British Museum, Sloane MSS, 3662, f.59.

[29] Noel Sainsbury *et. al.*, eds., *Calendar of State Papers, Colonial Series, America and West Indies* (hereafter *Cal. S. P. Col.*), 1661–8, pp. 528–9.

Willoughby estimated that the island did not furnish of its own growth 'one quarter Victualls sufficient for its Inhabitants nor any other necessaries for Planting . . .'.[30] By this time there was not one piece of unmanured ground large enough 'to draw a regiment of foot on without great damage'. Moreover, soil exhaustion, of which reports are extant as early as the 1660s, had apparently reached a critical point by the 1680s. The collection and application of dung, observed Edward Littleton, 'is a mighty Labour, which in effect is a Charge'. Terraces were built 'to stop the Mould that washes from our Ground; which we carry back into Carts or upon Negroes Heads. Our Negroes work at it like Ants or Bees'.[31]

For a synoptic view of the Barbadian economy, statistics have been compiled for the century, 1673–1773, showing changes in population and labour force, livestock, plantations, and export tonnage and values. Since data is lacking for certain years and certain categories and some of the figures are of doubtful accuracy, literary evidence will be drawn upon to supplement the data in Table III. Tonnage and value figures are five-year annual averages based on English imports and London wholesale prices. Official census returns which are used in this study commonly understate the actual slave population since planters concealed some of their slaves to avoid the poll tax.

Table III shows that the white population of Barbados declined to about 1710, after which it grew slowly to 1773 but not to the level of a century earlier. Despite the large migration in the early decades of the sugar industry, the island supported a larger white population than any of the smaller sugar colonies. By far the largest portion of the whites were indentured servants or smallholders who were settled on rent-free plots of marginal land by the wealthy sugar proprietors.

While the whites declined for a time and then increased slowly, the Negro population increased at an uneven rate and more than doubled in the course of the century. The ratio of whites to blacks declined from 1:1.5 in 1673 to 1:4.0 in 1773, which was on the high side compared with most of the sugar colonies. From literary evidence it may be presumed that a very high percentage of the slaves were engaged in sugar production and that the labour régime

[30] British Museum, Egerton MSS. 2395, f. 477.
[31] Edward Littleton, *The Groans of the Plantations* (1689), p. 16.

Table III

Barbados: Economic Structure and Trends, 1673–1773

	1673	1683	1710	1731	1748	1757	1768	1773
POPULATION								
White	21,309	17,187	12,525	16,113	15,252	16,772	16,139	18,532
Free Coloured					107		448	
Negro Slave	33,184	46,602	41,970	65,000	68,000	63,645	76,275	74,206
LIVESTOCK								
Horses/Mules			2,471	6,000			10,000[4]	
Horned Cattle				20,000			36,000[4]	
SUGAR PLANTATIONS								
Cattle Mills		358[2]	76		356[3]		19	14
Wind Mills			409	500			427	430
SUGAR EXPORTS								
Tons	6,950[1]		7,630	6,118	6,442	6,899	7,819	5,624
Value (£000)	250		267	122	219	264	287	200
TOTAL EXPORTS								
Value (£000)	350		477	219	392	472	513	357

NOTES: (1) 1655 (2) Sugar-works (3) 1750 (4) Author's estimates. Extensive use has been made throughout this study of quantitative data taken from contemporary sources. Though some of the data is probably of questionable accuracy, it does give some idea of the order of magnitude and can be roughly correlated with the literary evidence which is presented.

SOURCE: John Bennett, *Calculations on the Sugar Colonies* (1738), p. 19; John Campbell, *Political Survey of Britain* (1774), Vol. II, pp. 669, 673; Noel Deerr, *History of Sugar* (1949), Vol. I, pp. 166, 193; V. T. Harlow, *History of Barbados* (1926), p. 338; Griffith Hughes, *Natural History of Barbados* (1750), map following table of contents; John Oldmixon, *British Empire in America* (1708) Vol. II, pp. 162–3; Frank W. Pitman, *Development of British West Indies*, (1917) pp. 371–3; *Parliamentary Papers 1790*, Vol. XXIX, pp. 697–8

was most arduous. Père Labat, the French priest who visited Barbados in 1700, wrote:

> The English do not look after their slaves well and feed them very badly. As a rule the slaves are free to work on Saturday to provide themselves with all their own and their families' requirements. The overseers get every ounce of work out of them, beat them without mercy for the least fault, and appear to care far less for the life of a negro than for a horse ... The least disobedience is punished severely, and still more so are the slave risings.[32]

The decline in slave mortality during the eighteenth century points to some relaxation of the harsh labour régime described by Labat. Expressed as five-year annual averages, slave imports increased unevenly from 1,058 in 1691–5 to 4,573 in 1751–5, and to 5,101 in 1766–70, followed by a decline to 1,456 in 1771–5. In the period 1712–24, approximately 6 per cent of the slaves in Barbados had to be replaced annually to maintain the population, as compared with 3.8 per cent in the period 1765–75. If, as seems reasonable, it became less profitable to import fresh slaves from Africa than to breed slaves locally, then the ratio of working slaves to total slave population must have declined at the same time that maintenance charges increased as a percentage of total costs. In part, some of these added charges, especially foodstuffs, were met by shifting marginal cane lands into the cultivation of provisions.[33]

Horses and mules, and especially cattle, were needed to power mills, to draw carts and wagons, and to supply manure. In 1711, one inhabitant observed that 'without Cattle we can't make Sugar, for it is produced by dung and much labour'. George Washington described the making of dung during his visit to Barbados in 1751. Cattle were staked out on large heaps of loose earth and vegetable matter 'which they are three months trampling all the trash and then its fit to manure the Ground ... The very grass that grows amongst their corn is not lost but carefully gather'd for provender for their Stock!'[34]

---

[32] *The Memoirs of Père Labat 1693–1705*, tr. John Eaden (London, 1931), p. 126.
[33] Slave mortality and recruitment problems are discussed by J. Harry Bennett, Jr. in *Bondsmen and Bishops: Slavery and Apprenticeship on the Codrington Plantations of Barbados, 1710–1838* (Berkeley and Los Angeles, 1958), pp. 44–74, 136–41.
[34] *The Diaries of George Washington 1748–1799*, ed. John C. Fitzpatrick (New York, 1925), Vol. I, pp. 26–8.

Sugar planters replaced their cattle mills with wind mills, partly with a view to reducing the mortality of livestock. This change was well under way by the early eighteenth century when John Old-mixon wrote that 'lately every substantial Planter has one or two Wind-Mills, and some three, as at Sir Richard Hacket's, Sir Samuel Husband's, and Col. Drax's Plantations'. Table III shows that in 1683 there were 358 sugar-works, undesignated as to cattle or wind power. By 1709, Barbados had 1,309 'plantations' and 485 sugar-works, of which 409 were driven by wind and 76 by animal power. A total of 500 wind mills, each valued at £800, was reported in 1731, while in 1750 the number had declined to 356. Besides wind mills, planters purchased stills and earthenware pots to convert molasses into rum and muscovado or raw sugar into clayed or white sugar. By these and other means 'a rational management replaced by artificial means the former fertility'.[35]

After the seventeenth century, if not before, sugar estates were generally held by single proprietors and each estate had at least one mill. But some proprietors held two or more estates and some estates had two or more mills. Some idea of the complex land tenure system is afforded by Griffith Hughes's map of Barbados of 1750. It shows 238 sugar-planting families, 536 estates, and 356 wind mills. Indicative of the concentration of landed estates is the fact that 74 (or one-third) of the families, each holding three or more estates, held in the aggregate 305 estates, or 56.9 per cent of the total. Less than one-third (69) of the families, each with two or more mills, held in the aggregate 187 wind mills, or 52.5 per cent of the total. Among the great proprietary families were the Holders, Harrisons, Alleynes, Gibbs, Osbornes, Freres, Walkers, and Adams, each with six or more estates and four or more wind mills. It seems reasonable to conclude that of the 238 sugar-planting families, upwards of 70 were in an 'elite' category, having sufficient wealth and income to assume positions of political and social leadership in both colony and metropolis.[36]

Three estate inventories will convey some idea of the power- and capital-intensive nature of the Barbadian economy. John Sober

[35] John Oldmixon, *The British Empire in America* (2 vols. 1708), Vol. II, pp. 139–40, 151; Sir Robert Schomburgk, *The History of Barbados* (1848), pp. 140–1.
[36] Rev. Griffith Hughes, *The Natural History of Barbados* (London, 1750), map following table of contents.

left instructions in his will of 12 October 1751 that '200 negroes, 100 cattle and 10 horses to be kept on my estate, 60 acres to be planted in provisions, negroes to be well fed and clothed, and casks to be made'. Henley estate in 1762 consisted of 330 acres and 148 slaves. The land and buildings were appraised at £11,011, the livestock at £592, 48 men at £2,785, 48 women at £2,040, 28 boys at £947, and 24 girls at £625, total £18,000. George Frere said in 1768 that an estate of 250 acres required 170 Negroes, 100 horned cattle, 12 horses, 40 sheep, 3 tenants, a manager, a driver, two apprentices, a town agent, an apothecary, and a farrier.[37]

The extent to which sugar monoculture prevailed in Barbados may be seen by a breakdown of the island's exports in 1770. Expressed as a percentage of the value of total exports, sugar accounted for 56, rum and molasses for 37, and other products—chiefly ginger, cotton, and aloes—for 7. Sugar products thus constituted all but 7 per cent of the total. As for the division of exports between Great Britain and Ireland on the one hand, and North America on the other, approximately 72 per cent went to the former and 28 per cent to the latter. Comprehensive statistics are lacking for earlier years, but there is no reason to believe that—except in wartime—these ratios had altered significantly since the early years of the eighteenth century.[38]

V

Although Martinique is only about 150 miles to the northwest of Barbados, there are noteworthy differences in the geography and ethnology of the two islands which influenced their economic development. Barbados is a gentle rolling country with a coral limestone soil. The considerably larger island of Martinique is mountainous and has an active volcano; it has deep valleys and little flat land. A wider range of economic plants can be grown in the French island owing to variations in altitude and climate. Barbados has only temporary streams, while Martinique has many streams and rivers

[37] Vere L. Oliver, *Caribbeana* (London, 1919), Vol. v, p. 249; Bennett, *Bondsmen and Bishops*, p. 71; George Frère, *A Short History of Barbados* (London, 1768), p. 107.
[38] John Campbell, *A Political Survey of Britain* (2 vols. London, 1774), Vol. II, p. 669.

which powered its sugar mills. Barbados lies to eastward of the main chain of islands; its relatively isolated situation was an asset in time of war. Martinique is in the main chain of islands and in close proximity to other islands. Barbados was unoccupied when the first Englishmen arrived, while in Martinique the French fought bloody battles with the native Caribs before the island was secured. Compared with Martinique, slaves were less prone to rebel or run away in Barbados where there was a larger white population and less wasteland. When to these differences are added those in the mercantile systems of the mother countries, it is not surprising that the plantation economies of the two islands present interesting points of comparison.

Martinique was colonised in 1635 by a group of experienced planters from St Christopher. Numbering about one hundred, they were outfitted by Governor d'Esnambus of the mother island and directed to plant provisions, tobacco and other minor staples. While some progress was made in clearing and tilling the soil, the colonists were diverted by intermittent warfare with the Caribs until well into the 1650s. Partly for this reason, the colony was slow to attract settlers. They numbered about 1,000 in the early 1640s, and had increased to some 3,000 by 1660. Tobacco was the leading staple of the colony for several decades. But the depression of the tobacco market and crop limitation orders induced a number of settlers to turn to the cultivation of cotton, indigo, ginger, and roucou.[39]

Compared with Barbados, the sugar revolution in Martinique began later, extended over a longer period, and resulted in comparatively less displacement of small cultivators of minor staples and foodstuffs. In the 1640s an unsuccessful effort to cultivate and process sugar canes was made by one Trezel, a Dutch merchant of Rouen. Although a small quantity of sugar was made, the real beginning of the industry dates from 1654 when some 300 refugees from Brazil arrived on the island with their slaves and equipment. The leader of the group was a Jew, Benjamin Da Costa, who built two sugar mills and also established the first cocoa plantation. Even then the industry was slow to take root, for a number of the émigrés died of yellow fever or were attacked by Caribs. Colbert's efforts to drive out the Dutch and establish an exclusive French trading company

---

[39] Louis-Phillippe May, *Histoire Economique de la Martinique, 1635–1763* (Paris, 1930), pp. 1–75.

further impeded the industry. In fact, as late as 1671 there were only 12 sugar plantations and 14 mills on the island.[40]

After the period of slow growth, a quicker tempo characterised the industry in the last two decades of the seventeenth century. This is indicated by the statistics in Table IV. From 12 plantations in 1671, the number increased to 122 in 1683, 184 in 1687, and 207 in 1690. The population nearly trebled between 1678 and 1700 when the ratio of whites to blacks was little altered. Moreover, there was a doubling of the livestock population between 1683 and 1700. In part, the expansion can be attributed to changes in French colonial policy. By chartering a new African company, greater progress was made in supplying the planters with slaves. The establishment of three sugar refineries in Martinique was another innovation which greatly aided the planters for a few years. Meanwhile, the planters were learning to make semi-refined or clayed sugar which was encouraged by the home government after the refined product came under the ban.[41]

During the first three quarters of the eighteenth century the plantation economies of Barbados and Martinique exhibited several features in common. The Negro population increased more rapidly than that of the white, and at the end of the period the slave population of both islands was nearly equal. The number of sugar plantations increased for a time and then declined as planters enlarged their estates to take advantage of economies of scale. But it is apparent from Tables III and IV that the differences outweighed the similarities. The ratio of whites to blacks was substantially less in Martinique than it was in Barbados, while the former island had considerably more free coloured people. The livestock population of Martinique lagged behind that of Barbados, indicating less use of fertiliser in the French island. The sugar mills in Martinique depended primarily on cattle and water power, while those in Barbados came to be powered by wind. Martinique had many more small staple and provision plantations than did the neighbouring English island. Finally, the exports of Martinique came to be greater than those of Barbados, although the figures in Table IV overstate actual production owing to the not inconsiderable entrepôt trade of the French island. Less tangible differences include stricter crown regulation

---

[40] Canabrava, A Influéncia do Brazil na técnica do fabrico de açúcar', pp. 72–3.
[41] Guy Josa, *Les Industries du Sucre et du Rhum a la Martinique, 1639–1931* (Paris, 1931), pp. 71–82.

Table IV

Martinique: Economic Structure and Trends, 1671–1770

	1671–78	1683	1700	1709	1717	1736	1770
POPULATION							
White	2,450[1]		6,597	7,124	8,673	13,917	12,450
Free Coloured			507	733			1,814
Negro Slave	5,085[1]	9,384	14,566	20,282	23,000	55,692	70,996
LIVESTOCK							
Horses/Mules		1,200	3,668	6,478			8,283
Horned Cattle		5,200	9,217	11,205			12,376
SUGAR PLANTATIONS		122	183	246		447	286
Cattle Mills	12[2]						184
Water Mills	14[3]						116
Wind Mills							12
OTHER PLANTATIONS							
SUGAR EXPORTS							
SUGAR EXPORTS							1,515
Tons	120'[2]			5,719[4]	5,192	14,900	11,620
Value (£000)						560[5]	489
TOTAL EXPORTS							
Value (£000)						837[5]	881

NOTES: (1) 1678 (2) 1671 (3) Sugar-works in 1671 (4) 1710 (5) 1741

SOURCE: Noel Deerr, *History of Sugar* (1949) Vol. I, pp. 233–5: Guy Josa, *Les Industries du Sucre et du Rhum à la Martinique, 1639–1931*, (1931), pp. 69, 77, 94 and appendix; L. P. May, *Histoire Economique de la Martinique, 1635–1764*, (1940), p. 83; Public Record Office, C.O., 152/8, M76, E394, 35 (iv), f. 395; G. T. Raynal, *History of the East and West Indies*, tr. J. Justamond (1777) Vol. IV, pp. 154–5, 166–7.

of economic life in the French colonies, and the comparatively greater influence of the merchant class in Martinique.

Despite the substantial inflow of provisions from neighbouring islands, North America, and France, it seems evident that food crops were cultivated extensively in Martinique. No serious problem of provisioning the inhabitants occurred during the petty proprietor régime. But with the rise of sugar estates and slavery, planters were so avid for profits that they often failed to grow sufficient food crops for their slaves. The provisioning problem became more acute in the eighteenth century, especially in wartime when trade was interrupted, and on several occasions the island approached famine conditions. Unlike Barbados where the government adopted a *laissez faire* attitude, French officials in Martinique attempted to enforce minimum dietary standards, required planters to devote a certain portion of their lands to food crops, and freed slaves from plantation labour at least one day a week to cultivate their own provision grounds. Food crop statistics were recorded, as for example the report of 1736 which listed 4,806,142 banana trees, 34,583,000 trenches of cassava, and 247 plots of potatoes and yams. Although these measures met with some degree of success, it is the conclusion of Professor Debien that the French planters generally underfed their slaves.[42]

As with provisions, Martinique far outpaced Barbados in the cultivation of minor staples. We have seen that sugar monoculture prevailed in Barbados after the seventeenth century. On the other hand, Table IV suggests that minor staples made up from one-third to one-half of the value of Martinique's exports in 1736 and 1770. Together with provisions and livestock, these staples were grown on 1,515 plantations in 1770. While tobacco, the pioneer staple, had been abandoned before the end of the seventeenth century, cotton continued to assume considerable importance. Cocoa culture thrived for a time until disease practically destroyed the trees in 1727. But by then coffee trees had been brought to the island. Exports increased from about 328 tons in 1733 to 6,076 tons in 1753 to make coffee the second most important staple of Martinique.[43]

[42] G. Debien, 'La Nourriture des Esclaves sur les Plantations des Antilles Françaises aux XVIIè et XVIIIè Siècles', *Caribbean Studies*, Vol. IV, no. 2 (July, 1964), pp. 3–27.
[43] May, *Histoire Economique de la Martinique*, pp 87–103 and appendix

'The plantations, as they are called in Barbados, are far smaller than those in the French islands', observed Père Labat in 1700. 'This is not surprising because although the island is small, its population is very large, and as land is wanted by most of the inhabitants the plantations cannot be large, and the land is very valuable'.[44] Intensive agricultural practices were thus prevalent in Barbados, whereas the situation differed so markedly in Martinique that it was claimed in 1723 that one slave could cultivate as much land as two in Barbados. As expected, this productivity differential did not persist in the face of growing population pressure. Planters who had been able to patent more land than they had slaves to cultivate found that crown lands were diminishing and that they were granted on stricter terms. Whereas in 1680 planters had been allowed six years to bring their grants under cultivation, a declaration of 17 July 1743, confirmed to the governor-general and intendant the power to alienate all grants insufficiently cultivated.[45]

The sugar industry of Martinique grew extensively to about 1736, after which intensive culture became more prevalent. Extensive land use practices are suggested by the fact that the number of plantations increased about 2.5-fold between 1700 and 1736, while sugar production increased roughly in proportion to the slave population. The situation changed markedly from 1736 to 1770 when the number of plantations declined from 447 to 286. Sugar production rose to a peak in 1753 when 20,544 tons valued at approximately £805,615 sterling were exported (and re-exported). Thereafter, production and exports declined as the labour force engaged in sugar production appears to have increased.

As in Barbados, the planters of Martinique sought to mitigate the effects of diminishing returns by a variety of measures. Slaves were trained to replace white artisans, the quality of sugar was improved by the process called claying, estates were managed on a more rational basis, larger and more efficient plantation units were established, and more and more planters turned to water mills. On the other hand, the planters lagged far behind their Barbadian rivals in distilling their molasses by-product into rum. Then, too, one contempor-

[44] *The Memoirs of Père Labat*, p. 128.
[45] C. A. Banbuck, *Histoire Politique, Economique et Sociale de la Martinique sous l'Ancien Régime 1635-1789* (Paris, 1935), pp. 218–19.

ary noted that while soil exhaustion was widespread, few planters applied manure to their cane fields.[46]

'There are few who may be called midling people, they are either very rich or very poor . . .', observed George Washington during his visit to Barbados. Martinique was not unlike Barbados in having its very rich and very poor, but it also had a substantial group of 'midling' people. Abbé Raynal divided the proprietors of the lands on the island into four classes: rich people, planters in easy circumstances, those but little removed from indigence, and cultivators of small staples.

The first class possessed 100 large sugar estates in which 12,000 Negroes were employed.

> Their culture is carried to the highest degree of perfection, and they are able to preserve it in the flourishing state to which they have brought it. Even the expenses they must be at for replacing deficiencies, are not so great as those of the less wealthy planters, as the slaves born upon their plantations supply the place of those destroyed by time and labour.

The second class had 150 sugar plantations worked by 9,000 slaves. These planters were apparently caught in a vicious circle. Being understocked with slaves, their plantations did not produce enough income to support the credit they required to augment their labour force. The circle was even more vicious for the third class of sugar planters who possessed 30 plantations and 2,000 slaves. Finally, there were about 1,500 planters who employed 12,000 slaves in the culture of coffee, cotton, cocoa, and cassava. Compared with the third class, they required less assistance 'to recover that ease and plenty from which they are fallen, by war, hurricanes, and other misfortunes'. Altogether, Raynal estimated that a 'yearly accession of three thousand negroes' was needed to revive the declining plantations of Martinique.[47]

VI

After establishing bases in the Eastern Caribbean, England and France cast envious eyes on the Greater Antilles as a springboard to the

[46] Maurice Satineau, *Histoire de la Guadeloupe sous l'Ancien Régime 1635–1789* (Paris, 1928), p. 133.
[47] *Diaries of George Washington*, Vol. I, p. 29; Raynal, *History of the East and West Indies*, Vol. IV, pp. 169–71.

riches of Spanish America. Again, it was realised that military bases for attacking the Spanish colonies required economically viable colonies of settlement which combined subsistence and cash farming in support of military conquest, privateering, and trade. Accordingly, Cromwell launched his famous Western Design which, although unsuccessful against the Spanish colony of Hispaniola, succeeded in conquering the weakly-held island of Jamaica in 1655. The demographic pressure which induced thousands of northern Europeans to migrate to the Lesser Antilles to engage in small staple production, was followed by the sugar revolution and the consolidation of tobacco and cotton farms into plantations worked by Negro slaves. Many redundant planters and indentured servants in St Christopher, Nevis, and Barbados joined the expedition which conquered Jamaica. Other Frenchmen, Englishmen, and Dutchmen had earlier occupied the small island of Tortuga. From here they crossed the narrow body of water to Hispaniola, first engaging in hide hunting and tobacco growing, and then, in retaliation to Spanish military pressure, to buccaneering. The upshot was French intervention on behalf of the buccaneers and the cession by Spain to France in 1697 of the western third of the great island of Hispaniola or St Dominigue.

Despite favourable environmental conditions, agriculture made only limited progress in Jamaica and St Domingue. For some years there were quicker roads to wealth. Wild cattle lured the hide hunter, abundant forests the logwood cutter, Spanish gold and silver the buccaneer, illicit trade the merchant.

As religious wars gave way to dynastic and imperial struggles, the West Indies became the cockpit of European rivalry. While the Spanish colonies continued to be a major target of attack, northern European nations began to vie with one another for possession of plantation colonies, slaves, and other moveable property. The English colonies were especially vulnerable to French raiding parties during the wars of the seventeenth century. One such party under Admiral Du Casse invaded the eastern parishes of Jamaica in 1694, burning cane fields, destroying over fifty sugar-works, and carrying off to St Domingue some 1,900 slaves.

Planters not only feared attacks from without, but also the escape and rebellion of their slaves from within. Mountainous and unsettled areas in both colonies attracted runaway slaves, or Maroons, who raided frontier plantations and fomented unrest among estate Negroes.

In St Domingue the gree coloureds were employed as rangers in clearing the woods and mountains of Maroons, while in Jamaica there was a long and costly war which involved British troops, local militia, and Mosquito Coast Indians prior to the Maroon Treaty of 1739. Slave insurrections were less frequent in the period prior to 1791, largely owing to more stringent police regulations which Professor Goveia says 'lay at the very heart of the slave system'.[48]

It is not surprising that plantations were slow to take root when to these and other difficulties are added the head start of the smaller islands. Nevertheless, the drawing power of cheap and fertile land was not to be denied. Economic plants and livestock had been brought to the Greater Antilles by the Spaniards. From the Lesser Antilles came experienced planters with their servants, slaves and equipment. Immigrant capital was supplemented by trade credit and loans from European merchants who traded with the Caribbean colonies. Moreover, if the experience of Sir Henry Morgan and Admiral Du Casse is any guide, no little capital for settling plantations came from the buccaneers who terrorized the Spanish Main from their strongholds at Port Royal and Tortuga.

At the time of the English conquest the Spaniards in Jamaica grew cotton, cocoa, tobacco, grapes, sugar, and foodstuffs, besides grazing large herds of swine, goats, and cattle. Few commodities other than hides and tallow were exported. While the cultivation of foodstuffs was necessary to avoid starvation, the first generation of Englishmen made only limited advances in commercial agriculture. One contemporary said that by 1671 the island contained 42 cocoa walks, 19 indigo works, 57 sugar and 3 cotton plantations, besides a number of small plantations. Cocoa was the leading staple until 1671 when the trees were destroyed by disease. Meanwhile, sugar had gained a foothold by drawing on experienced planters from the eastern Caribbean. Governor Modyford's arrival on the island in 1664 with some 800 settlers from Barbados is said to mark the real beginning of the industry. In 1675, a resident said there were '20 sugar works that make 150,000 lbs. to 200,000 lbs. of sugar per annum,

---

[48] Elsa V. Goveia, 'The West Indian Slave Laws of the Eighteenth Century', *Revista de Ciencias Sociales*, Vol. IV, no. 1 (March, 1960), p. 82. The plundering and looting of plantations was especially acute in the Dutch colony of Surinam during the 1760s and 1770s, at a time when there were as many as 5,000 or 6,000 Maroons. Radjnarain M. N. Panday, *Agriculture in Surinam 1650–1950* (Amsterdam, 1959), pp. 26–30.

Table V

Jamaica: Economic Structure and Trends, 1673–1774

	1673	1684	1703	1739	1754	1768	1774
POPULATION							
White	8,564	9,000[1]	7,000	10,080	12,000	17,949	18,420[4]
Free Coloured							4,100[5]
Negro Slave	9,504		45,000	99,239	130,000	166,914	205,261[4]
LIVESTOCK				84,313[3]		135,773	
Ranches				34			500
SUGAR PLANTATIONS	57	70[2]		429		648	775
Cattle Mills						369	
Water Mills						235	
Wind Mills						44	
OTHER PLANTATIONS				230			998
SUGAR EXPORTS							
Tons	670	3,586	4,337	16,016	20,845	36,021	50,000
Value (£000)			180	460	724	1,322	1,750
TOTAL EXPORTS							
Value (£000)			287	652	1,025	1,871	2,400

NOTES: (1) 1677 (2) 1675 (3) 1740 (4) 1778 (5) 1775

SOURCE: John Campbell, *Political Survey of Britain* (1774), Vol. II, p. 666; Noel Deerr, *History of Sugar* (1949), Vol. I, pp. 176, 198; Bryan Edwards, *History of British West Indies* (1793), Vol. II, p. 466; Edward Long, *History of Jamaica* (1774), Vol. I, p. 301; Frank W. Pitman, *Development of British West Indies* (1917), pp. 373–8; George W. Roberts, *Population of Jamaica* (1957), pp. 33–6.

about 50 that make 100,000 lbs., and more in great forwardness'.[49]

A comparative view of Barbados and Jamaica in the century from 1673 to 1674 is afforded by the data in Tables III and V. In terms of sugar exports, Jamaica forged ahead of Barbados in the early years of the eighteenth century; she was consistently ahead after 1725, and by 1771-5 the margin had widened to a ratio of ten to one. Unlike Barbados, the sugar plantations of Jamaica increased in number throughout the century. No less obvious was the growing disparity in the labour force, livestock population, and export values of the two islands. Then, too, Jamaica differed from Barbados in having numerous cattle ranches and minor staple and provision plantations.

Despite its much larger Negro population, Jamaica failed to out-pace Barbados in the size of its European population. The Maroon War was both cause and effect of the growing disparity between the whites and blacks, for the war itself made frontier settlements un-safe, and thus discouraged immigration, while the slaves were em-boldened to revolt by the paucity of white masters. Considerable efforts were made to come to grips with the dilemma: colonisation schemes calling for liberal land grants and subsidies were set on foot, while 'deficiency' laws levied stiff penalties on planters who failed to maintain a proportionate number of white servants to Negro slaves. Colonists and indentured servants responded to these meas-ures, it is true, but on such a limited scale that the white population of Jamaica lagged behind that of the slaves until the ratio was one to eleven in 1774.

The twenty-fold increase in the slave population during the cen-tury from 1673 to 1774 came in response to the profitable nature of sugar production. That the profits were higher in Jamaica than in the smaller islands was the contention of one inhabitant who wrote that 'a sugar work with 60 negroes will make more profit than one with 100 in any of the Carribbees, the soil being new, and well shaded with goodly woods.'[50]

Compared with the smaller islands, Jamaica made heavier demands on the people of Africa after the early decades of the eighteenth century. Expressed as annual averages, the number of imported slaves

[49] *Cal. S. P. Col.* 1675-6. Appendix 1574-1674, p. 314.
[50] *Idem.*

(less those re-exported) increased unevenly from 2,989 in 1706–10, to 7,210 in 1751–5, and to 8,069 in 1771–5. Not all of the imports added to the population because of the high mortality. Writing in 1788, Hector M'Neill said that the planters of Jamaica had formerly considered their slaves as 'so many cattle' who continued to perform their dreadful tasks for seven or eight years, and then expired. In a modern study Dr Roberts estimates that the annual rate of natural decrease was nearly 4 per cent in the period 1722–34, and that before 1776 it fell below 2 per cent in only one period (1734–9).[51]

Although low in an absolute sense, dietary standards were probably higher in Jamaica than in Barbados. This seems a reasonable judgement in view of comparative mortality estimates, as well as the source and nature of Negro provisions. Whereas Barbados was to a large extent a foreign-fed island, with widely fluctuating and highly perishable food imports, Jamaica was better supplied with ground provisions from its ample land reserves. The slaves in the latter island were normally allotted one and half days each week for their own activities, during which time they cultivated plots set aside by their masters for growing provisions. On many estates they had small plots—kitchen gardens—near their slave quarters and larger plots in outlying parts of the estate. There was an element of truth in the assertion of one white inhabitant that

> what renders their slavery tolerable to them, is that little shadow of property and freedom which they seem to enjoy, in having their own little parcels of ground to occupy and improve; and a great part of its produce they bring to market, there to dispose of it; which, besides supplying the white inhabitants with a great plenty of wholesome provisions, enables the negroes to purchase little comforts and conveniences for themselves and their little ones.[52]

Historians of peasant agriculture and local markets find the antecedents of these institutions in the slave-plantation era.

As with slave provisions, Jamaica was less dependent upon imported supplies of livestock than its sister island. For one thing, Jamaica

---

[51] Hector M'Neill, *Observations on the Treatment of Negroes in the Island of Jamaica* (London, 1788), pp. 4–5; George W. Roberts, *The Population of Jamaica* (Cambridge, 1957), p. 37.
[52] *An Enquiry Concerning the Trade, Commerce, and Policy of Jamaica* (Jamaica, 1757), pp. 32–3; see also Sidney Mintz and Douglas Hall, 'The Origins of the Jamaican Internal Marketing System', *Yale University Publications in Anthropology*, no. 57 (1960), pp. 3–26.

had extensive savannas which were well suited to grazing but lacked sufficient moisture for tillage. Moreover, the quality of the grazing lands was improved by the introduction of Guinea Grass from Africa in 1744. Livestock not only grazed on pastures included in sugar estates, but separate ranches of 'pens' became numerous in Jamaica. Some of the pens were owned by sugar planters, while others were operated as independent grazing units. Livestock use patterns also differed widely: fertiliser requirements were relatively greater in Barbados, whereas transport and mill power requirements were relatively greater in Jamaica.[53]

While provisions and livestock expanded in response to the growing sugar industry, no such trend is evident for minor staples until coffee became an important production of Jamaica after 1783. According to an inventory compiled by Edward Long, in 1751 there was a total of 205,800 acres in inferior staples and breeding pens, made up of cotton works, 15,400; pimento walks, 6,000; ginger plantations, 4,400; provision plantations, 72,000; and breeding pens, 118,000. Long railed at the sugar planters who had patented far more land than they could cultivate, or had formed plantations by swallowing up by degrees 'all the little settlements around'. He urged the legislature of Jamaica to encourage poor and industrious persons to cultivate cocoa, ginger, aloes, coffee, and pimento—all of which 'require no great labour, are not burthensome in the carriage, and which have a sufficient demand at home, to recompense those who do not look for vast and sudden fortunes'.[54]

But most Jamaicans were in search of the vast and quite sudden fortunes which sugar promised after the riotous days of buccaneering had subsided. Since landed estates were the basis of such fortunes, grants of public land became objects of intense rivalry, the prizes being awarded to the strong, the rich, and the politically influential. Already by 1670 there were 47 individuals who held 1,000 acres or more (or 42.5 per cent of the patented lands). Accession to the planter oligarchy continued in subsequent decades. In fact, the Quit Rent Book for 1754 lists 467 individuals (or 29.2 per cent of the patentees), who held between 1,000 and 22,000 acres (or 77.8

[53] Douglas Hall, *Free Jamaica 1838–1856, An Economic History* (New Haven, 1959, London, 1969), pp. 13–17.
[54] Long, *History of Jamaica*, Vol. I, pp. 385, 495, 513.

per cent of the patented lands). At the other extreme were 263 individuals who held less than 100 acres.[55]

Seventeenth century plantations were confined largely to the south-central plains region of Jamaica which was accessible to the ports of Fort Royal, Kingston, and Old Harbour and less vulnerable to attack by land and sea. After the Maroon War, however, plantations spread to outlying parts of the island, increasing from 429 to 775 between 1739 and 1775. Extensive land-use practices, which were of limited applicability on long-settled estates, now became feasible. In fact, the new lands which were cleared for cane cultivation were commonly worn out by incessant cultivation. After wearing out one piece of land, the planters were said to 'pass on to a new piece, which is destined to be worked to the bone in the same manner; and very few of them understand the method of preparing suitable com-posts for their land'.[56] Jamaica's sugar plantations thus differed markedly from those in the smaller islands, being more land-intensive on the one hand, and less labour- and capital-intensive on the other hand.

Even in the long-settled parishes the sugar estates varied so widely in area and equipment that it is hazardous to generalise about the intensity of cultivation. Professor Piman has analysed the census data of 1753 for St Andrew or Liguanea Parish. This parish adjoins the port of Kinsgton on the south coast, being about 15 miles broad and 12 miles in depth.

> The total number of estates in the parish in 1753 was 154. They range in size from the little truck garden of Benjamin Israel containing three acres, ten slaves, and two head of cattle, to the broad acres of Philip Pinnock, the show place of Jamaica, containing 2,872 acres of which 242 were under sugar cane yielding 140 hogsheads a year, and equipped with 16 white servants, 280 slaves, and 326 head of cattle.

Of the 154 estates in the parish, 128 produced no sugar but were engaged on a moderate scale in raising provisions, coffee, ginger, livestock, and cotton. In total acreage the 26 sugar plantations ranged from 257 to 2,872, in cane acreage from 5 to 310, in white servants from 1 to 16, and in Negroes from 30 to 280. Eight estates had no land devoted to provisions and pasture. On the remaining estates provision acres ranged from 10 to 250, and pasture or pen from 4 to

[55] *Cal. S. P. Col.* 1669–74, pp. 99–103; Public Record Office, London, C.O. 142/31.
[56] Long, *History of Jamaica*, Vol. I, pp. 440–1.

1,000. On the other hand, 16 estates had woodlands which ranged from 33 to 1,100 acres. Sugar monoculture was the rule, for only 3 of the 26 estates had small acreages devoted to coffee, ginger, and cotton.[57]

Slave population and valuation data have been compiled by the author from the personal property inventories in the Jamaica Public Record Office. In the period 1741–5, when 69 sugar estate inventories were recorded, the median estate had a total of 99 slaves, valued at £21 5s sterling each, made up of 32 men at £29 16s, 34 women at £20 9s, and 33 children at £13 15s. In the period 1771–5, when 97 inventories were recorded, the median estate had 204 slaves, valued at £37 6s sterling each, made up of 73 men at £48 11s, 71 women at £38 6s, and 60 children at £22 18s. These samples point to a more than two-fold increase in slave population and a 3.5-fold increase in total slave valuation on a median sugar plantation in Jamaica.[58]

By the standards of its time the typical Jamaica plantation was truly a big business unit in terms of labour force, industrial equipment, and capitalised value. Valued at approximately £19,300 sterling, the median plantation in 1774 had roughly two-fifths of this capital invested in Negro slaves, slightly less than a third in land and growing canes, about one-fifth in processing equipment, 7 per cent in livestock, and 2 per cent in utensils.[59]

Although comparable statistics are lacking, it seems evident that Barbadian plantations were smaller in area but of relatively higher capitalisation. A visitor to Barbados in 1717 said that the planters divided their cane lands into thirds—one third standing canes, another third new-planted canes, and the other third fallow. 'In Barbados they plant every crop or second crop; in the other islands they have ratoons, or second, third, fourth, &c. crops from the same roots, but every succeeding year they yield less'. Furthermore, he said: 'They allow one good field negro for one acre canes, all labour included. The labour is very considerable (supposing the ground

[57] Frank W Pitman, 'The Settlement and Financing of British West India Plantations in the Eighteenth Century', in *Essays in Colonial History Presented to Charles McLean Andrews by his Students* (New Haven, 1931), pp. 261–70.

[58] Jamaica Public Record Office, Spanish Town, *Inventorys*, Vol. 26, ff. 29–31; Vol. 50, ff. 177–9 Jamaica currency values are converted into sterling at the ratio of 1·4 to 1 in these computations.

[59] See Table I, p. 100.

well cleared and brought to) viz. holeing, planting, dunging, weeding, hilling, and cutting'.[60] It thus seems clear that while the economy of Barbados was one of intensive-monoculture, that of Jamaica should be properly described as one of extensive-monoculture.

However much the two islands differed in intensity of production, no great difference separated them in terms of sugar monoculture. Expressed as a percentage of the value of Jamaica's exports in 1770, sugar accounted for 76, rum and molasses for 13, and other products —chiefly mahogany, pimento, cotton, coffee, and ginger—for 11. Whereas 89 per cent of Jamaica's exports consisted of sugar products, the percentage for Barbados was 93. The Jamaicans differed from the Barbadians, however, in making proportionately less rum to sugar and less clayed sugar to muscovado sugar. They also sent proportionately less of their exports to North America (10 per cent), and proportionately more to Great Britain and Ireland (90 per cent).[61]

VII

No plantation society presents such vivid contrasts as the French colony of St Domingue. Nature endowed it with beautiful scenery, richness of soil, and salubrity and variety of climate. Man transformed its alluvial plains into fields of waving sugar-canes; he denuded its richly forested hills and mountains to grow cocoa and coffee. It became the scene of troops of Africans toiling under a vertical sun, presided over by lordly planters and their retinues of white and mulatto servants. The term 'plantation' connotes many opposites: the planter's great house and the miserable mud and wattle hut of the slave, green cane fields turned red by the torch of rebellious slaves, ships bringing new recruits from Africa to replace those who died prematurely, other ships taking away the products of slave labour to sweeten the repast of the European. White and black, green and red, sweet and bitter, opulence and poverty, leisure and labour, submission and rebellion—these were the contrasting elements which culminated in the great slave revolt and the destruction of the wealthiest plantation society in the Americas.

[60] William Douglass, M.D., *A Summary, Historical and Political, of the British Settlements in North America* (2 vols. London, 1760), pp. 117–18.
[61] Campbell, *Political Survey of Britain*, Vol. II, p. 666.

Starting later than the other French and British colonies, St Domingue forged ahead of its chief rival, Jamaica, in the second quarter of the eighteenth century. Table VI shows that between 1739 and 1775 its white population increased nearly three-fold and its slave population more than doubled. Between 1720 and 1775 its sugar exports increased in tonnage by nearly five-fold, while in the latter year total exports amounted to about £4 million sterling, one half of which was sugar. Moreover, in 1775 St Domingue exceeded Jamaica by 77 per cent in the number of whites, 72 per cent in free coloureds, 22 per cent in Negro slaves, 18 per cent in sugar exports, and 67 per cent in the value of all exports to Europe.

But, as with Rome, no plantation society was made in a day. In the pioneer period some of the hide hunters and logwood cutters had settled down to grow tobacco. After a time they were joined by immigrants who found it profitable to cultivate cotton, indigo, and cocoa. Cocoa thrived for a time until the trees were ravaged by disease in 1715. St Domingue owed its first real prosperity to indigo which was the leading export in the early part of the eighteenth century. Indigo and coffee required substantial investment in processing equipment; they were much like sugar in that the production unit was both a farm and a factory, albeit generally on a smaller scale. Coffee was introduced from Martinique by the Jesuits and was first grown successfully in 1738. Its culture spread rapidly in the mountainous parts of the island and in the course of a few decades it came to rank second only to sugar. Whereas minor staples constituted only about 11 per cent of Jamaica's exports in 1770, approximately 37 per cent of the exports of St Domingue fell in this category in 1767, made up of coffee 17.5 per cent; indigo 12.6 per cent; cotton 6.0 per cent; hides 0.8 per cent; cocoa 0.3 per cent; and carette 0.1 per cent.[62]

'My Lords, the French begin to tred upon our heels in ye Sugar trade. They have better Islands I assure your Lordships than Wee, and St Domingue will in time be a vast settlement'. Governor Codrington wrote this letter to the Board of Trade from Antigua in 1701, at a time when the sugar industry of St Domingue was in its infancy. In that year there were said to be 35 mills at work grinding cane, with 25 more ready to crush, and nine partly constructed.

---

[62] Pierre Leon, *Marchands et spéculateurs dauphinois dans le monde antillais du XVIIIe siècle Les Dolle et les Raby* (Paris, 1963), p. 204.

Table VI

St-Domingue: Economic Structure and Trends, 1681–1775

	1681	1710	1720	1739	1754	1767	1775
POPULATION							
White	4,336			11,540	14,253		32,650[3]
Free Coloured					4,911		7,055[3]
Negro Slave	2,312			117,411	172,188	256,776	249,098[3]
LIVESTOCK							
Horses/Mules					63,454		75,958
Horned Cattle					92,946		77,904
SUGAR PLANTATIONS		55[1]		350	599	544	648
Raw Sugar					344		385
White Sugar					255		263
OTHER PLANTATIONS							2,587[4]
SUGAR EXPORTS							
Tons		2,920	10,500	42,400[2]		62,640	59,226
Value (£000)						1,936	1,993
TOTAL EXPORTS							
Value (£000)					1,261	3,194	4,069

NOTES: (1) 1701 (2) 1742 (3) 1779 (4) Indigo-works only

SOURCE: Noel Deerr, *History of Sugar* (1949), Vol. I, p. 240, Vol. II, p. 280; Pierre Leon, *Marchands et spéculateurs dauphinois dans le monde antillais du XVIIIe siècle Les Dolle et les Raby* (1963), pp. 196–209; Jacques Necker, *De l'administration des finances de la France* (1784), Vol. III, chap. 13; G. T. Raynal, *History of the East and West Indies*, tr. J. Justamond (1777), Vol. IV, pp. 228–9; G. T. Raynal, *Histoire . . . des Europeens dans les Deux Indes* (1781), Vol. VII, pp. 134–6, and table opposite page 210; Pierre de Vaissiere, *Saint-Domingue* (1629–1789), (1909), pp. 21, 164.

Père Labat visited the colony in 1701 and remarked on the depth and fertility of the soil near the port of Du Cap on the north coast. 'In truth it is a lovely country and should prosper. The settlers are beginning to make sugar instead of indigo which has been cultivated up to that time'. In the parish of Leogane near Port-au-Prince, Labat visited a large plantation belonging to Governor Du Casse who had acquired great wealth in the sacking of Cartagena and the raids on Jamaica. 'The settlers all gamble to excess, live very well, and vie with each other in displaying their wealth'.[63]

St Domingue forged ahead of Barbados, Martinique, and Jamaica in the early decades of the eighteenth century. 'There are already more than 200 sugar-works and the number increases daily', wrote Pierre Charlevoix, the Jesuit traveller and historian, in 1724.

> Each factory makes an income of 30,000 *livres*, without counting the molasses and cane brandy, which are worth more than a 1,000 crowns. If one multiplies 30,000 by 200 it will be seen that the Plain de Cap produces each year 6,000,000 *livres* in sugar, and that will be increased by one-third [i.e. by the by-products].[64]

By 1739 St Domingue had approximately 350 plantations producing upwards of 40,000 tons of sugar annually; in the colony as a whole there were a reported 11,540 whites who directed the labour of 117,411 Negro slaves.

Although its commanding position was maintained until the slave revolt of 1791, the colony's sugar industry experienced fluctuating fortunes. After the initial surge the pace slackened for several decades after 1739, at least by comparison with Jamaica. Whereas Jamaica's sugar exports increased by 34,000 tons between 1739 and 1744, those of St Domingue increased by 18,000 to 20,000 in the same period. Paradoxically, St Domingue's labour force outpaced that of its leading rival by some 26,000 slaves in the period from 1739 to 1774. There are several possible explanations of this paradox. For one thing coffee estates may have absorbed a growing portion of the labour force. Another possible explanation is that the two wars of this period retarded the French sugar industry while that of the British colonies experienced little disruption. But probably an even

[63] Public Record Office, London, C.O. 152/4, E51, f. 106; *The Memoirs of Père Labat*, pp. 148, 159, 165.
[64] Pierre Charlevoix, *Histoire de l'isle espagnole où de Saint Domingue* (Paris, 1730), quoted in Deerr, *History of Sugar*, Vol. I, p. 239.

weightier factor was the diversion of labour and other resources to the construction of irrigation projects, water mills, and roads.

So rapid was the expansion of cane acreage that planters faced declining yields as the most productive lands in the colony approached exhaustion. Though fertile soil was in relatively abundant supply, the level and seasonal distribution of precipitation presented problems of great difficulty. Some areas lacked adequate rainfall, while others were plagued with faulty distribution, rapid evaporation, and frequent flooding. Yet there were numerous streams and several large rivers which had adequate watershed areas in the mountains to maintain stream flow when alluvial plains areas were parched for lack of moisture. Frenchmen in St Domingue were not slow to realise that plantation expansion depended on costly investments in water control projects. In many ways the French were uniquely fitted for such an undertaking. The mother country had an excellent school of civil engineering, and advances were being made in hydraulics and hydraulic engineering. Not a few of the engineering graduates were army officers who were posted in St Domingue. In time some of these officers married sugar heiresses or in other ways became proprietors of plantations. Together with able public officials, these officer-planters mobilised support for ambitious irrigation projects.[65]

Beginning in about 1730, the Dominguans constructed a highly developed irrigation system using surface waters. Most of these projects were undertaken in the west and south—on the Artibonite Plain, Cul-de-Sac Plain, and Cayes Plain—where irrigation was generally imperative. Only on the North Plain was precipitation generally sufficient to preclude the need for irrigation. Syndicates of planters undertook these projects under the paternal eye of government. Engineering plans were drawn up and approved, funds were raised, slave labour was pledged, and water rights apportioned. The construction called for the building of reservoirs, diversion dams, levées, and aqueducts, and the cutting of canals and ditches. Some of the projects met with insurmountable obstacles as was the case on the Artibonite Plain where floods broke through the levées on repeated occasions. On the other hand, the works on Cul-de-Sac Plain were highly successful. Altogether, upwards of 100,000 acres

[65] Pierre de Vaissiere, *Saint-Dominigue La Société et la Vie Creoles sous l'Ancien Régime (1629–1789)* (Paris, 1909), pp. 93–154.

were in irrigation districts by the end of the colonial period.[66]

Benefits in the form of higher cane yields far outweighed the construction and waiting costs. Near the end of the colonial period Moreau de Saint-Méry travelled from parish to parish and described the irrigation works in great detail. Concerning the Cul-de-Sac projects, he wrote: 'On estime que cette grande entreprise a cause une dépense de trois millions; mais aussi, combien de millions elle assuré!'[67] Bryan Edwards, the Jamaica planter-historian, was another visitor who was impressed with the agro-engineering achievements of the French. He estimated that the French lands yielded nearly two-thirds more than 'all the land in canes throughout Jamaica'. This difference arose partly from superior fertility, 'and, above all, from the prodigious benefit which resulted to the French planters from the system of watering their sugar-lands in dry weather. This is an advantage which nature has denied to the lands in Jamaica, except in a very few places'.[68]

Contributing to increased agricultural productivity were other factors. The same engineering works which brought water to the cane fields were adapted to the requirements of water wheels until most of the cattle mills were replaced by the superior energy source. Moreover, French engineering genius found expression in the construction of bridges and all-weather roads which reached into every part of the level plains and into the smaller adjacent valleys. Besides land transport, some of the lower reaches of the rivers were made navigable, thus enabling planters to transport their bulky staples to the major seaports. An advantage of another type which St Domingue had over Jamaica was ready access to imported supplies of livestock, provisions, and specie from Spanish Hispaniola. 'They supply them with stockings, hats, linnens, guns, hard ware and some wearing apparel', wrote Raynal, 'and receive in return horses, horned cattle both for slaughter and for labour, smoked beef and bacon, skins, and lastly, twelve or fifteen hundred livres'.[69]

[66] French irrigation works are described by John S. Brown, 'Water Resources', in *Geology of the Republic of Haiti*, by Wendell P. Woodring, *et. al.* (Port-au-Prince, 1924), pp. 517–38.

[67] Mederic L. E. Moreau de Saint-Méry, *Description Topographique, Physique et Historique de la Partie Française de l'Isle Saint-Domingue* (3 vols. Paris, 1958), Vol. II, p. 945.

[68] Bryan Edwards, *An Historical Survey of the French Colony in the Island of St. Domingo* (London, 1797), pp. 136–7.

[69] Raynal, *History of the East and West Indies*, Vol. IV, p. 231.

Productivity increments from the engineering works went chiefly to the class of great planters. These projects so increased yields that in some instances the value of land was more than doubled. Since sugar enjoyed a comparative advantage over other staples on the fertile and irrigated plains, it was to be expected that the great staple should reign supreme in these areas. This is borne out by Moreau de Saint-Méry whose survey shows that while a number of indigo and cotton estates were irrigated, by far the greater number were sugar estates (*sucreries*). Irrigation and water power not only increased the value of cane lands; they also called for the relocation and reconstruction of sugar works and additional land and Negro slaves to take advantage of economies of scale.

The rewards and hazards attending the irrigation of plantations in St Domingue have been documented with great care by Professor Debien. Among his numerous case studies is that of 'La Sucrerie Contineau', covering the period 1750–77. This plantation, belonging to the Cottineau family, was situated in the northeast corner of the colony near the port of Fort-Liberté and adjacent to the river Marion. The plan was to extend a partly completed canal in order to irrigate cane fields and power the sugar mill. Although water rights were secured in 1758, actual construction was delayed by the uncertainties of war and the need to acquire additional land and slaves. When work commenced in about 1770, the digging of the canal and irrigation ditches was only part of the undertaking. There were also the costly and time-consuming tasks of relocation and reconstruction. Numerous buildings had to be shifted and rebuilt, including the slave quarters, hospital, great house, and sugar works. Cane fields and provision grounds had to be rearranged without too much disturbance to the normal plantation routine.[70]

Lacking a complete inventory of Cottineau before 1784, only certain aspects of the expansion can be shown. In 1753, there were 133 Negro slaves, consisting of 39 men, 23 women, 25 girls, 22 infants, and 24 who were old and infirm. In the same year there were 25 horses and 38 head of horned cattle. The estimate of 8 July 1784, on the other hand, listed 173 slaves, of which 60 were men, 65 women, 26 boys, and 22 girls. Livestock in the latter year consisted of 75 mules, 9 horses, and 66 head of horned cattle. Table VII summarises the estimate of 1784 in English units.

[70] G. Debien, *Plantations et Esclaves à Saint-Domingue* (Dakar, 1962), pp. 32–43.

Compared with the medium-sized plantation in Jamaica (Table I, p. 100), Cottineau was much larger in area and capitalised value, although the latter is probably exaggerated by the rise in the price level in both islands from 1774 to 1784. On the other hand, Cottineau had 31 fewer slaves and 24 fewer head of livestock at the same time that values per slave and per head of livestock were considerably higher. The outstanding difference, however, was the highly assessed value of the cane lands which reflected the capitalised value of the irrigation works on Cottineau in contrast with the unwatered estates in Jamaica.

Table VII

Estimate of 'La Sucrerie Cottineau', St Domingue, 1784

	Number	Average Value*	Total Value*
Total Acres	1,560	£15 7s	£23,950
(Acres in Canes)	(453)	(44 2s)	(19,983)
Sugar Works			9,593
Negroes	173	48 14s	8,423
Livestock	150	16 4s	2,427
Utensils, etc.			774
Total			£45,167

* St Domingue livres are converted into sterling at the ratio of 28·7 to 1.

SOURCE: G. Debien, *Plantations et Esclaves à Saint-Domingue* (Dakar, 1962), p. 18.

The correspondence quoted by Professor Debien shows that no little effort was made to increase the labour force during the years of reconstruction. Both imported and 'seasoned' slaves, but chiefly the former, were purchased: 20 in 1766, 16 in 1767, 7 in 1769, 28 in 1773, 7 in 1774, 51 in 1775, and possibly others. But the same letters which notified the absentee proprietor of new purchase also informed him of deaths and runaways. The manager complained that slave merchants imported few Gold Coast Negroes who were superior workers and many Congolese who fell ill easily and died prematurely. Among other causes, Negro deaths were attributed to contagious disease, accidents, poisoning, and suicide. Moreover, the extra labour required to dig canals and rebuild the sugar works contributed to the high mortality. The plantation doctor and nurses fought a losing battle with the grim reaper. Underfeeding caused other slaves to escape across the border into Spanish Hispaniola. Indeed, the loss was so great that new purchases equalled and perhaps exceeded the average of about 150 slaves on Cottineau. 'Autrement dit, de 1765 a 1778, l'atelier a été entièrement renouvele'.[71]

If Cottineau made extraordinary demands on the people of Africa, the experience of other plantations was not much better. Irrigation and other improvements, it is true, increased yields, but these gains by no means saved either the labour or the importation of slaves. On the contrary, they encouraged planters to engage in extravagant speculations, to drive their Negroes to produce more staples and thus build up a retirement fund in the metropolis. Pierre Victor Malouet, himself a planter in St Domingue before 1773, estimated that the mortality was two or three times greater than that of any other country on earth.[72] The increase in the slave population from about 170,000 to 480,000 between 1750 and 1790 shows that it was not enough to merely fill the ranks of those who fell. Indeed, slave imports increased from 3,667 in 1720, to 5,200 in 1753, to between 10,000 and 15,000 from 1764 to 1767, and to upwards of 30,000 just two years before Toussaint L'Ouverture sounded his clarion call in 1791. 'Let the colonies be destroyed rather than be the cause of so much evil,' said the *Encyclopedia* in its article on the slave trade.[73]

VIII

The foregoing discussion has traced the elements of uniformity and diversity which made the West Indian plantation an absolutely unprecedented social, economic, and political institution. We have

---

[71] *Ibid.*, pp. 44–51, 56–76.
[72] *Essai sur St Domingue*, pp. 148 ff., quoted by Henry Brougham, *An Inquiry into the Colonial Policy of the European Powers* (2 vols. Edinburgh, 1803), Vol. II, pp. 536–7.
[73] Quoted in C. L. R. James, *The Black Jacobins Toussaint L'Ouverture and the San Domingo Revolution* (New York, 1963), p. 24.

seen that hoe cultivators and artisans from Africa were combined with European technology and management, American and Asiatic plants, and American soil and climate. Efforts were made to bring these elements together in least cost combinations, first in a small island setting, and then overflowing into the Greater Antilles and rimland areas. Economic development progressed from gathering the products of forests and savannas and subsistence agriculture, to small staple culture, and the cultivation and processing of great staples. Nevertheless, the pattern of development varied widely in time and place, being influenced by such factors as resource endowments, imperial policy, market fluctuations, wars, and natural disasters. Small farms and plantations coexisted with great plantations, small staples with great staples, subsistence crops with export staples. Sugar plantations ranged widely in acreage, labour force, livestock population, energy scources, land use practices, and capitalisation. At one extreme were the small, intensively cultivated estates of Barbados, at the other the latifundia of Jamaica and St Domingue. Moreover, there were significant differences between the French and British colonies with respect to crop diversification and public works projects.

Market distance and perishability, among other factors, made it necessary for staples to undergo certain processing, grading, and packaging operations in the West Indies. Tobacco was cured and graded, indigo was placed in vats of water which released the dye from the leaves, coffee berries were cured, dried, and milled to separate the husks from the beans. Coopers assembled staves, hoops and headings into barrels, puncheons, tierces, and hogsheads to package the staples for export.

'More than any other kind of plantation in the West Indies', writes Professor Pares, 'sugar production combined industry and agriculture'.[74] Not only did the industrial establishment comprise the fixed structures and equipment, but it also included the white and Negro artisans—boilers, distillers, coopers, carpenters, masons, wheelwrights, and millwrights. By the middle years of the eighteenth century few planters continued to employ white artisans. In fact, one planter insisted that the Negroes, even those imported from Africa, learned the different trades 'with as much facility and perseverance

[74] Pares, 'Merchants and Planters', pp. 23–4.

as the white people do in Europe'.[75] When the capital invested in Negro artisans, whose appraised value was often twice that of field hands, was added to the value of the sugar works and utensils, the industrial capital amounted to nearly half the total value of the plantation.

The sequence of operations consisted of preparing the soil, planting, weeding, harvesting, crushing, boiling, curing, and distilling. No sooner was one task completed, or partially completed, than another demanded the attention of the planter and his slaves. The tempo hardly abated during occasional slack seasons in the sugar routine, for subsidiary operations, such as provision culture and maintenance of buildings and equipment, occupied the field hands and artisans. Samuel Martin, the Antigua planter, likened a sugar plantation to 'a well constructed machine, compounded of various wheels, turning different ways, and yet all contributing to the great end proposed, but if any one part runs too fast or too slow in proportion to the rest, the main purpose is defeated'.[76] Given the need for careful timing and coordination, it is not surprising that the industrial-type labour of the mill pervaded the workers in the field. 'The discipline of a sugar plantation is as exact as that of a regiment', wrote James Ramsay, 'at four o'clock in the morning the plantation bell rings to call the slaves into the field. Their work is to manure, dig, and hoe, plow the ground, to plant, weed, and cut the cane, to bring it to the mill, to have the juice expressed, and boiled into sugar'.[77] The planter was at once a landlord, a farmer, and a manufacturer; his plantation was truly an agro-industrial enterprise.

Similarly, plantations were agro-commercial and financial enterprises. They were profit-making business units commonly organised as single proprietorships and calling for initiative and judgment by the owner or manager. Much of the planter's time was taken up with securing market and exchange information, buying and selling, negotiating loans and credits, hiring shipping space and insurance, and keeping records. Indeed, large planters were so taxed to keep

---

[75] William Beckford, *A Descriptive Account of the Island of Jamaica* (London, 1790), Vol. II, p. 351; Richard B. Sheridan, 'Planter and Historian: The Career of William Beckford of Jamaica and England', 1744–1799, *The Jamaican Historical Review*, Vol. IV (1964), pp. 49–55.

[76] Samuel Martin, *An Essay Upon Plantership* (Jamaica, 1802), p. 57.

[77] James Ramsay, *An Essay on the treatment and conversion of African slaves in the British sugar colonies* (London, 1784), p. 69.

abreast of their business affairs that they required managers or over-seers to supervise plantation operations, writers to copy business letters, bookkeepers to keep accounts, town agents to transact local business, and commission agents in the metropolis to handle a variety of trading and financial matters. 'The trade of planting', observed Lord Brougham, 'though connected with the soil, is yet, from the extent of the capital required in it, from the rapidity of improvement, from the large profits and the constant risk ... much more nearly allied to commerce than to agriculture, and promoted by the spirit of mercantile adventure'.[78] Surviving letter books and plantation ledgers point unmistakably to the spirit of mercantile adventure.

Since plantations, especially sugar plantations, were great farms and factories with an industrial labour régime and a pronounced market orientation, it is pertinent to enquire about the social origins of the men who owned and managed these estates. Were the great planters of the mid-eighteenth century period the descendants of transported criminals, indentured servants, yeomen farmers, the gentry, the lesser nobility, or peers of the realm? Were they descended from buccaneers and freebooters, merchants and factors, artisans, government officials, military officers, or members of the learned professions? There is no easy resolution of the question of social origins, partly because all classes and conditions of men contributed to the planter oligarchy, partly because conditions varied from colony to colony and even in the same colony the social origins of the planters changed over time, and partly because of the planter's propensity to identify wealth with noble ancestry and to consciously dissociate themselves from their humble forebears.

The origins and activities of the leading planter families of Antigua in the period 1730–75 have been investigated by the author. Of the 65 families studied, 36 were of English or Welsh decent, 13 Scottish, 7 Irish, 1 each of Dutch and French extraction, and 7 unascertained. Approximately 36 of the 65 families came to Antigua between 1632 and 1680, some from the colonies of St Christopher, Barbados, and Surinam, and others directly from the British Isles. They consisted of planters, both large and small, retired soldiers and sailors, former shipmasters and buccaneers, government officials, lawyers, doctors, merchants, and artisans. In the vanguard were the

[78] Brougham, *Colonial Policy of the European Powers*, Vol. II, pp. 159–60.

locally-based merchants, traders, and factors who were strategically based to transform mercantile capital into plantation capital. Few of the planter families were without mercantile connections, either by origin or intermarriage. During the eighteenth century a number of Scots lads gained entry into the Antigua gentry largely through their mercantile ties and medical skills. Numbered among the 65 families in the period 1730–75 were 29 local merchants, 20 London-West India merchants, 14 lawyers, 18 doctors, 12 members of parliament, 1 lord mayor of London, and 9 titled persons. Instead of the planters being a distinct class, it is more appropriate to regard them as merchant-planters or planter-merchants. Moreover, the Nonconformist origins of the Antigua gentry was quite pronounced, including the Scots Presbyterians, the Puritan family of Winthrop, and the Quaker family of Langford.[79]

There is little reason to believe that the planter elite of Antigua differed essentially from that of other British sugar colonies. The Royalists who fled to Barbados in the Civil War period may have given that colony an aristocratic element of some importance. But few Royalists were apparently unsullied by the taint of trade, for a number of them were reported to have accumulated plantation capital by serving as storekeepers for Dutch merchants. French planters were probably recruited to a greater degree from the army, civil service, and lesser nobility. Yet the researches of Professor Debien show that the *petite bourgeoisie* merchants played a predominant part in the colonisation and plantation development of the French Antilles. Indeed, the mercantile influence tended to increase rather than to decrease, since the growing burden of debt compelled more and more planters to convey their estates to merchant creditors.[80]

The mercantile nature of the plantation colonies was in part a reflection of European rivalry for the wealth of the New World. In the sixteenth century Portugal and Spain had laid claim to outlying parts of the world and under a rigid system of state control had amassed great wealth from spices and precious metals. Coming late in the race for the colonial jackpot, the north Europeans resorted to war and freebooting to siphon off the wealth of the Iberian empires. At

[79] R. B. Sheridan, 'The Rise of a Colonial Gentry: A Case Study of Antigua, 1730–1775', *Economic History Review*, 2nd ser., Vol. XIII, no. 3 (1961), pp. 342–57.

[80] G. Debien, *Une Plantation de Saint-Domingue La Sucrerie Galbaud du Fort 1690–1802* (Cairo, 1941), pp. 33–4.

the same time efforts were made to foster industry, shipping, trade, and colonisation, and by means of a favourable balance of trade, to draw bullion from the empires to the south. Since the founders of plantation colonies were merchants actively engaged in privateering ventures and relatively free from mercantile restrictions, it is not surprising that colonies were valued in large measure by the private trading profits that they yielded. Even after colonial compacts came into being, there was more scope for private trade by nationals of the northern countries than was permitted by the Iberian nations.

The rise of the plantation colonies must be seen against the background of major economic and social recession and secular adjustment which has been termed 'the crisis of the seventeenth century'.[81] The collapse of Spain and her imperial economy in America was only one aspect of the crisis since there were also such tenuously related areas of breakdown as the Mediterranean, southwest Germany, and the Baltic hinterland. In both England and France there was a pronounced slowing down in industrial development and trade after 1620, complicated by the disorders of the Thirty Years' War and the English Civil Wars. Subsequently, economic relationships were disrupted by the Anglo-Spanish War which led to the conquest of Jamaica, the three Anglo-Dutch Wars, and the Franco-Dutch War.

From infant colonies of little consequence in councils of state, the West Indies began to loom large in the north European design for maritime power and wealth after the advent of the sugar revolution. Having been frustrated in their efforts to maintain intra-European trades in an age of crisis, the merchants of England and France turned to the plantations and, with the aid of government, ousted the ubiquitous Dutchman. The shift from Europe to America was no temporary phenomenon, for trade with the plantation colonies grew more rapidly than other branches of trade for a century or more.

Gradually there developed a relationship with the plantations which was truly an engine of economic growth for the metropolis and its colonies in North America. The combined and constant labour of slaves in conjunction with European technology and management yielded a steady output of tropical goods which found grow-

---

[81] E. J. Hobsbawm, 'The General Crisis of the European Economy in the 17th Century', *Past and Present*, nos. 5 & 6 (May and November, 1954), pp. 33–49, 44–63.

ing markets in Northern Europe and North America. Conversely, slave-plantations became captive markets for a wide variety of European manufactures, for intermediate products from the temperate-zone colonies to the north, and indirectly for the goods that were sent to Africa to purchase slaves. Plantation colonies also became entrepôts for licit and illicit trade with Spanish America; European manufactures and African slaves were traded for bullion, livestock, cochineal, and other staples. The West contributed to trade with the East, for Spanish bullion flowed through Northern Europe to the Orient where it purchased spices, tea, calicoes, and ornamental wares. Semi-processed staples and raw material from the West Indies required ample shipping capacity so that great fleets were constructed to engage in shuttle trades and tramp voyages. Sugar refineries and cotton mills were established in the metropolis to process the colonial staples. Thus, within the framework of Atlantic empires there developed complementary, reciprocal, and multilateral trading patterns which gave rise to regional specialisation, interdependence, and growth.

IX

Sharply contrasted with the plantation economy of the north European was that of the 'hacienda' or large landed estate of the Spaniard in the New World. Whereas the plantation was a prime factor in Northern European recovery from the crisis of the seventeenth century, the hacienda was both cause and effect of the decline and decadence of imperial Spain from the early seventeenth century to the revival under the Bourbon monarchs more than a century later. New World Spaniards responded to the collapse of the mining boom and consequent decline in overseas trade by establishing quasi-feudal and relatively self-sufficient landed estates which served chiefly local and regional markets. By their failure to develop export industries based on resources other than minerals, they thus contributed to the moribund state of the metropolitan economy. But first a few remarks about the origin and nature of Spain's colonial society.

Coming to the New World more than a century before the north Europeans, the Spaniards established a colonial society which reflected the feudal, military, and clerical institutions of the homeland

in contact with the lands and peoples of America. In a real sense the conquest of America was a sequel to the long centuries of military and religious crusading against the Moors which culminated in the reconquest of Spain. The first arrivals were chiefly natives of the poor upland regions of Castile who as soldiers had participated in the Reconquest, and as civilians were essentially drovers, shepherds, and miners. Though common folk by origin, military life had imbued them with the values of the hidalgo, or lesser noble. They were fighters and rulers who disdained manual labour. They were motivated by dreams of gold, hopes of glory, and visions of God. Given such values and social background, it is not surprising that conquering, robbing, ranching, and mining were their chief economic activities, and that after the fabulous discoveries of gold and silver in Mexico and Peru, precious metals were the staple exports of Spanish America.

Notwithstanding the military character of the first arrivals, some interest was shown in agriculture. Necessity drove some Spaniards to tilling the soil, while others were men of influence who by the *repartimiento* system were given a weekly allotment of Indians to work the land, and by the *encomienda* the right to collect tribute through local chiefs. Not only was much learned from the tillage practices of the Indians, but efforts were made to introduce domesticated plants and animals and to adapt European agriculture to the American environment. Large estates were first established in the pioneer colony of Española at a time when the gold mines were nearly exhausted and many Spaniards were following the conquistadores to Mexico and Peru. In part, these were cattle ranches which exported hides and tallow. Then for several decades the sugar industry assumed some importance in Española. Six sugar mills were in production by 1625. The number rose to 34 in the late 1630s when the legal exports of sugar amounted to about 1,000 tons annually. Since the Indian population had been virtually destroyed by disease and forced labour in the mines, the planters turned to African slaves to man their estates. But the slave trade did not flourish, and chiefly for this reason the sugar industry of Española collapsed suddenly in the mid-1570s.[82] By this time the island settlements of Española, Cuba, Jamaica, and Puerto Rico had become

[82] Mervyn Ratekin, 'The Early Sugar Industry in Española', *Hispanic American Historical Review*, Vol. XXIV, no. 1 (February, 1954), pp. 1–19.

sparsely populated pastoral economies, the greater portion of their inhabitants having been lured to the continent by promises of gold and glory.

From the Spanish conquest between 1519 and 1520 down to the mid-eighteenth century period, the economic history of New Spain (Mexico) falls into three broad phases. First came the silver cycle from about 1530 to 1630–40, next came the rise and maturing of the hacienda, and finally there were such developments as the revival of mining and reform of the imperial system, chiefly in the second half of the eighteenth century. The first establishments of the conquistadores were primarily military in character, drawing surplus agricultural produce from the Indians by means of encomiendas and repartimientos. The silver cycle did much to stimulate agricultural and pastoral colonisation since the miners required quantities of foodstuffs, draft animals, and hides; the ships which carried the treasure to Spain needed provisions; and thriving markets developed in centres of administration—chiefly in Mexico City.

The rise of the hacienda can be best understood against the background of economic decline which set in after the first silver cycle. Broadly speaking, the decline was a consequence of Spain's failure to reorganise her imperial economy along complementary lines. Conceivably, precious metals might have been used to expand the manufacturing industries of the metropolis and the agricultural staples of the colonies so that a base for sustained trade would have been established before the mines were exhausted. The failure to realise such an imperial economy was due in part to misguided policy, in part to Spain's resource base, climate, and culture. Since subtropical commodities, including cane sugar, were grown in southern Spain, there was apparently little incentive to develop plantation colonies in America. In fact, Spain remained primarily a producer of foodstuffs and raw materials—chiefly wine, olive oil and wool. Gains in manufacturing were quickly erased by the influx of American treasure, for costs and prices rose earlier and more rapidly in Spain than in north Europe, and Spanish merchants turned to the cheaper sources of supply to make up cargoes for the colonies. Other difficulties stemmed from the lack of slave trading posts in Africa, onerous restrictions on colonial trade and shipping, and the failure to restrict certain branches of manufacturing in the colonies. Professor Hamilton maintains that the influx of American gold and silver created an illusion of prosperity, and that this euphoric attitude was partly responsible for 'the aggressive foreign policy, contempt for manual arts, vagrancy, vagabondage, luxury and extravagance, which led to the economic decadence of the seventeenth century'.[83]

As the vital links of overseas trade and shipping weakened, Spanish America withdrew into itself and developed an economy which was only peripherally dependent upon the mother country. The tonnage of ships plying between Spain and the Indies declined by about 75 per cent during the first three quarters of the seventeenth century, while the diminished cargoes consisted largely of manufactures from Northern Europe.

Similarly, the legal exports of colonial staples were reduced to a mere trickle at a time when clandestine trade from the foreign-held islands in the West Indies took on added dimensions. Parelleling and complementing the decline in overseas trade was the marked slow-down both in inter-colonial and intra-colonial commercial life. In Mexico the natural propensity of the Spaniard toward dispersal had been accentuated by the discovery of mines in remote provinces. The collapse of the mining boom left widely scattered centres of population that were far removed from the seaports and inter-connected by primitive roadways. 'Each region and even each locality tended to become isolated and self-sufficient and to huddle under the authority of the large landowners or local leaders', writes Professor Chevalier.[84]

We have seen that plantations, situated in island and rimland areas of low elevation and sparse population, relied on the labour of imported African slaves. Haciendas, on the other hand, were confined largely to continental tropical or subtropical highland regions and depended on the labour of American Indians. The Spaniards who first conquered Mexico were attracted to plateau areas (*Meso-america*), where there was a large Indian population. Here the sedentary Indians used only the fertile and well-watered parts for their maize-bean-squash culture. Having no domesticated animals except the dog, the Indians had no use for the vast tracts of sub-

---

[83] Earl J. Hamilton, 'The Decline of Spain', *Essays in Economic History*, ed. E. M. Carus-Wilson (London, 1954), Vol. I, p. 224.
[84] Francois Chevalier, *Land and Society in Colonial Mexico, The Great Hacienda* (Berkeley and Los Angeles, 1963), p. 49.

humid grasslands which the Spaniards appropriated for cattle and sheep-grazing *encomiendas*. During the sixteenth and early seventeenth centuries the Spaniards claimed the right to tribute and labour from the Indians. But the Indians were so decimated by disease and hard labour in the mines that the religious orders appealed to the Crown to eliminate all forced labour. Gradually, the system of colonial labour progressed from Indian slavery, to limited labour services under the *repartimiento* system, and finally to free labour except for the limited number of Negro slaves. Meanwhile, feudal land tenure arrangements were giving way to private ownership and large landed estates began to encroach upon Indian settlements. Land appropriation was one means of forcing the 'free' Indian to seek employment on the great estates. Landed proprietors also attracted the natives to settle on their estates by advancing sums of goods and money which the Indians could never pay back in labour services. Debt peonage, or serfdom through debt, thus ensured a combined and constant labour force which grew cash crops for the owner and subsisted itself to a large extent from family provision grounds. Debt peonage became a full fledged institution in the seventeenth century under the hacienda economy.[85]

The common image of the hacienda is one of a landed estate extending to thousands of acres and devoted to cattle grazing, the administrative centre consisting of the great house (*casa grande*) of the patron and his many relatives, the crude adobe houses of the peons, a chapel with a resident priest, a commissary store, and numerous outbuildings and corrals. This picture is quite characteristic of much of Spanish America in the period of this study. Cattle haciendas, which used little labour and capital, and much land, spread over the vast spaces separating the population centres of Mexico and gave the country its most distinctive institution. However, sheep grazing haciendas, which supplied wool to the colony's weaving mills, increased relative to cattle haciendas after the mining demand for livestock products subsided. In fact, many of the richest landed proprietors were sheep raisers, and it was not uncommon for these haciendas to be run in conjunction with weaving mills.

[85] *Ibid.*, pp. 13, 36–7, 49, 64–9, 265–9, 285, 288, 295; John P. Augelli, 'The Rimland-Mainland Concept of Culture Areas in Middle America', *Annals of the Association of American Geographers*, Vol. LII, no. 2 (June, 1962), pp. 119–29; Silvio Zavala, *New Viewpoints on The Spanish Colonization of America* (Philadelphia, 1943), pp. 93–103.

Moreover, in scattered areas of fertile and well-watered land there were numerous wheat haciendas, sometimes operated in conjunction with flour mills. Other estates in tropical and subtropical portions of Spanish America combined the features of haciendas and plantations and produced such marketable staples as indigo, cocoa, cotton, and sugar.

Sugar estates in seventeenth century Mexico combined some features of the plantations of northern Europeans with other characteristics of Spanish haciendas. In both areas the farm and factory were generally single units of ownership and control, although independent refinery units were more common in Mexico. In both areas Negro slaves performed heavy field labour and tasks requiring some degree of skill, but in Mexico they were greatly outnumbered by Indian labourers. Production for the market was characteristic of both areas, but the Mexican plantations supplied local and regional markets chiefly.

Sugar planters in Mexico were frequently absentees as were their counterparts in the Caribbean, but they were attracted to Mexico City rather than to Europe. For the most part, however, the Mexican sugar estate was more akin to the hacienda in its remoteness from tropical lowland areas and in accessibility to ocean transport, its self-sufficiency in foodstuffs, building materials, and livestock, its dependence upon local supplies of labour and local and regional markets, and its patron-peon relationship which emphasised paternalism, power, prestige, and prodigality almost to the exclusion of pecuniary calculation. So self-sufficient were the largest sugar plantations of Mexico that they had pastures capable of grazing many hundred head of pack animals, working oxen, and cattle and sheep to supply the Indian and Negro population with meat, leather, and wool. Planters preferred cooler inland valleys to lowland coastal areas, partly for reasons of health and well-being, partly to grow maize and wheat on fields of higher elevation than the sugar canes, partly to draw fuel from woodlands, and partly to utilise streams for mill power and irrigation. Besides the sugar mills, large estates were equipped with woollen mills, flour and grist mills, forges, and workshops.[86]

After 1650 the moribund state of the Spanish empire was accentuated by the rise of northern European countries and their

[86] Chevalier, *Land and Society in Colonial Mexico*, pp. 71, 74–83, 289–95.

plantations in the West Indies. By 1700 Spain was reduced to 'the lowest depths of decadence', with an army of 20,000 men, a fleet of only 20 vessels, and an empty treasury. 'The population of some 6 million souls dwelt in misery in a country without roads, without commerce, without agriculture, and without industries'.[87] By contrast, the 'ever increasing importance of colonies' to the northern countries was said to have resulted from the more general use in Europe of sugar, tea, and coffee. In fact, the productions and trades of the West Indies were so important in the years from 1700 to 1740 that 'more than one state regarded them as the foundation of their commercial, and even their political, greatness'.[88] William Pitt, the great commoner, is said to have 'had a vision of a stream of commerce flowing from the various ends of a vast empire. Great Britain was to be the brains of this body politic, and the West Indies the heart through which the life-blood flowed'.[89]

The northern powers not only drew wealth from their tropical plantations, but they also dominated the colonial trades of the Iberian countries. In part, the trade was conducted indirectly through Cadiz and Lisbon by resident English and French merchants; in part, it was a direct and largely contraband trade that was conducted through such entrepôts as Kingston, Jamaica. By 1763 France had a slight lead over Britain in the indirect trade which swallowed up the greater part of the bullion entering Spain through legal channels. On the other hand, Britain held a preponderant share of the direct trade, having overtaken the Dutch contraband traders in the early decades of the eighteenth century. British domination was enhanced by the trading privileges she enjoyed in Spanish America as the holder of the Asiento slave contract, and by her military victories and conquests during the War of Jenkins' Ear and the Seven Years' War. Nearly four hundred ships were reputedly employed by the British in the contraband trade during the latter war, at a time when the Spaniards used scarcely ten in the legitimate traffic. Indeed, the French ambassador in Madrid claimed that the British made

---

[87] Herbert I. Priestley, *José de Gálvez Visitor-General of New Spain 1765–1771* (Berkeley, 1916), p. 13.

[88] A. H. L. Heeren, *A Manual of the History of the Political System of Europe and its Colonies*, tr. Henry G. Bohn (London, 1830), pp. 172, 199.

[89] Kate Hotblack, *Chatham's Colonial Policy* (London, 1917), p. 70.

far more profit from the Spanish Empire than did the Spaniards themselves.[90]

Realising that a colonial policy of monopoly and bullionism had been a dismal failure, Spain turned to the reform and rehabilitation of her imperial economy in the eighteenth century. The first effort to revive the Empire by pooling the resources of Spain and France proved abortive, for the Bourbon alliance antagonised England and resulted in military defeat and trade encroachment during and following the War of Spanish Succession. Nevertheless, the Bourbon powers continued their reform efforts, being drawn together more closely by Britain's growing seapower in Atlantic and Caribbean waters. Taking the mercantilist policies of Colbert as a guide, Spain proceeded step by step to expand home industry, to rebuild her merchant marine and navy, to suppress contraband trade, to break the Cadiz monopoly of the colonial trade, and to reform colonial administration and finance. Colonial monopoly was not abandoned; rather it was liberalised in an effort to make the Empire economically viable and thus restore Spanish maritime and military power.

The interesting thing is that Spain's efforts were directed to the Greater Antilles and tropical rimland of the Caribbean rather than to the inland plateaus of Mexico and Peru. Moreover, the development of slave-plantations and trade in agricultural staples was given precedence over that of mines and haciendas.

Beginning in 1728, three joint-stock companies were chartered by the Spanish government and granted trading monopolies with island and rimland colonies. Cocoa was cultivated by some 750 haciendas in Venezuela when the Caracas Company sent its first ships to the colony in 1728. The Company's first task was to oust the Dutch contraband traders who dominated the Spanish Main from their island-fortress in Curacao. Professor Hussey says that the Caracas Company found Venezuela a poverty stricken province and left it prosperous, having played a major role in expanding production and trade in cocoa and tobacco. In the Greater Antilles the Havana Company was chartered in 1740 to handle the trade, and especially the tobacco monopoly, of Cuba. The Company achieved some degree of success in expanding tobacco and sugar production, suppressing

[90] Allan Christelow, 'French Interest in the Spanish Empire During the Ministry of the Duc de Choiseul, 1759–1771', *Hispanic American Historical Review*, Vol. XXI, no. 4 (November, 1941), p. 532; J. H. Parry and P. M. Sherlock, *A Short History of The West Indies* (London, 1957), pp. 95–126.

contraband trade, and reviving trade with the mother country. The Barcelona or Catalan Company was chartered in 1755 for trade with Santo Domingo, Puerto Rico and other islands outside the Havana Company's sphere. On the whole the Company's performance was disappointing, although it did contribute to the future expansion of Puerto Rico by importing 9,450 Negroes into that island from 1766 to 1770.[91]

Except for the port of Havana, Cuba experienced little economic development until the second half of the eighteenth century when it emerged as the first full-fledged plantation colony in the Spanish empire. From the conquest in 1511–12, the island had a succession of industries which were from time to time its main dependence; namely, gold, hides, tobacco, coffee, and sugar. The gold seeking and mining phase was both short-lived and of limited yield, yet it witnessed the virtual extinction of the native Indians. Negroes were imported as early as 1523, but for a century or more the island's slave population was probably not in excess of one thousand. As with the other Spanish Antilles, Cuba lost the greater part of its colonists during the rush to the continental mining frontiers. Then for approximately two centuries the island was little more than a great pasture land outside the immediate vicinity of Havana and Santiago de Cuba. Livestock haciendas occupied the greater part of the sparsely populated island, from which were exported hides, skins, and a little tobacco. Hindering the development of plantations were such factors as the island's vulnerability to wartime incursions and freebooters, restrictive mercantile policies, lack of technical skills, capital, and managerial ability, and, above all, the uncertain supply and high prices of African slaves.

Cuba's sugar industry, though it dates from 1547 when the first *trapiche*, or horse-powered mill, was constructed, did not make much progress until the third quarter of the eighteenth century. The number of *ingenios*, or water mills, increased from between 50 and 70 in the late seventeenth century, to 120 in 1765, and to 473 in 1775. Sugar exports to Spain, which amounted to about 2,000 tons in 1640, rose to 5,200 tons in 1765, and to 8,200 tons in 1771.

[91] Roland D. Hussey, *The Caracas Company 1728–1784* (Cambridge, Mass., 1934), pp. 52–70, 74, 86–9, 178–81, 207–17, 233–4, 299–300.

West Indian plantations were creations of northern European countries at a time when a growing portion of the population had disposable income for purchase of non-European goods, when sparsely populated tropical islands were accessible to sailing vessels, when international mobility of production factors—labour, capital, and entrepreneurship—made it possible to establish raw-material export industries in areas of fertile tropical soils, when private property rights were extended over peoples of preliterate culture, and when European firearms supplied the ultimate sanction for a régime of forced labour. Moreover, relatively high yields were realised by combining such inanimate converters as wind mills and water mills with Negroes, the most numerous, available, and strongest slaves. By contrast with the Orient where Europeans found established centres of production and trade, West Indian plantations were artificial economies created for the express purpose of trade, navigation, and seapower. First established in a period of acute social and economic crisis, the plantation set in motion a cumulative process of economic development which linked together temperate and tropical areas of the Atlantic and Caribbean world and drew into its orbit the wealth of the Iberian empires. Plantation America was an integral part of European capitalism in the 'Age of the Commercial Revolution'. The plantation was at the vortex of dynamic forces—some creative and others destructive—which culminated in slave revolts, anti-slavery movements, and political and industrial revolutions in North America and Northern Europe. More than any other factor, the extension of plantations depended on slave or indentured labour which was tied to the land. So destructive to life and well-being was this labour system in most parts of the tropical world that insuperable political obstacles have been erected to bringing men and land together in plantation units. Plantation history thus goes far to explain the revolutionary impact of Western civilisation and the revolt of non-Western peoples against Western ascendancy.

An era of West Indian prosperity
1750-1775

An era of West Indian prosperity
1750-1775

Voltaire, in his widely-read novel *Candide,* tells of the encounter of Candide with a Negro slave in the colony of Surinam. Finding the Negro lying on the ground, half clothed and lacking a left leg and a right hand, Candide exclaimed: 'Oh, my God! What are you doing there in that horrible state?' Whereupon the Negro replied: 'When we are working in the sugar refineries and a finger is lost in the mill, the whole hand is cut off; when we try to escape, a leg is cut off. I have suffered from both these practices. This is the price paid for the sugar you eat in Europe'.[1]

As with other leaders of the Enlightenment, Voltaire sought to alert his generation to the social costs of plantation produce by dramatising the horrors of slavery. There is no doubt that he threatened a formidable array of economic and political interests. 'The most approved judges of the commercial interests of these Kingdoms have ever been of opinion that our West Indian and African trades are the most beneficial that we carry on', asserted an anonymous English writer. Planters received

> a constant supply of Negroe servants for the culture of their lands in the produce of Sugar, Tobacco, Rice, Rum, Cotton, Fustick and Pimento and all other Plantation Produce, so that the extensive employment of our shipping in, to, and from America, the great Brood of Seamen consequent thereon, and the Daily Bread of the most considerable Part of our British Manufactures, are owing primarily to the Labour of Negroes.

The writer concluded that the Negro trade, 'and the natural consequences resulting from it may justly be esteemed an inexhaustible Fund of Wealth and Naval Power to this Nation'.[2]

---

[1] *Oeuvres complètes de Voltaire,* (52 vols. Paris, 1877–85) Vol. XXI, p. 180.
[2] Anon., *The national and private advantage of the African Trade considered* (London, 1749).

I

Professor Pares has denominated the period between the Peace of Paris (1763) and the outbreak of the American Revolution as the 'silver age of sugar', the 'golden age' having occurred a century or more earlier when the sugar industry was launched in the Lesser Antilles under conditions of low costs, high yields, and prices which, while falling, were much higher than those of any subsequent period. While the intervening period was marked by fluctuations in the staple industries of the West Indies, a dominant feature of the Atlantic economy was Europe's capacity to absorb growing quantities of tropical produce at prices which were remunerative to the white agents of production.[3]

Adam Smith said that Europe benefited from the discovery and colonisation of the New World, 'first, in the increase of its enjoyments; and secondly, in the augmentation of its industry'. From the New World came a variety of commodities which Europeans would not have otherwise possessed, 'some for conveniency and use, some for pleasure, and some for ornament, that thereby contributes to increase their enjoyments'. From the vantage point of France, Abbé Raynal noted that the nations which had acquired possessions in the West Indies had, 'by fortunate circumstances, or by well-combined projects, become the residence of the arts, and of all the polite amusements which are a natural and necessary consequence of great plenty'.[4]

Apart from France and England, comparative data on the consumption of tropical goods is difficult to find. Frenchmen probably consumed more coffee, cocoa and indigo than their neighbours across the channel. On the other hand, French sugar consumption (imports less re-exports) in 1775 was less than two-fifths of that of England and Wales, or 30,000 tons as compared with 80,200 tons. 'If the wealth of *France* was as great or as generally diffused, that is, if the mass of their people were as thoroughly employed, and

[3] Richard Pares, 'Merchants and Planters', *The Economic History Review*, Supplement 4 (Cambridge, 1960), p. 40.
[4] Adam Smith, *An Enquiry into the Nature and Causes of the Wealth of Nations* (New York, 1937), p. 557; Abbé Raynal, *A Philosophical and Political History of . . . the East and West Indies*, tr. J. O. Justamond, (8 vols. London, 1788), Vol. v, pp. 353–4.

thereby as easy in their circumstances, as the bulk of the *British* nation actually are, they would then of course consume much more [sugar] and export far less', was the judgment of one Englishman. French sugar re-exports in 1775 amounted to about 51,000 tons, or 63.0 per cent of the colonial product entering the metropolis.[5]

The drinking habits of Englishmen and Frenchmen influenced sugar consumption both directly and indirectly. A London merchant stated in 1724: 'The Consumption of Sugar in England, by the great use of Tea or Coffy is very much encreased, of late, expecially by the cheapness of Tea which will alwise enlarge the Consumption'. Fifty years later Edward Long, the Jamaica planter-historian, attributed the 'prodigious augumentation' in the home consumption of sugar to 'the low prices of teas for some years past'. Besides tea, rum-punch became a popular drink in England and North America, whereas in France these two beverages made few inroads on wine and brandy.[6]

London and Paris sugar prices indicate that the demand tended to run ahead of the supply from the mid-1730s to 1775. Barbados muscovado sugar sold at the London Custom House rose irregularly from an average price of 16s 11¼d per hundredweight in 1733 to 32s 0½d in 1747, and fell to 27s 9½d in 1750. During the third quarter of the century, when there was a slightly upward trend, the price never fell below the 1751 figure of 30s 6d, and reached a high point of 45s 9d in 1759. Expressed in Livre Tournois, Paris sugar prices rose from 12.5 per hundredweight in 1736 to 25.1 in 1747, thereafter falling to 14.0 in 1752. They moved upwards irregularly to 29.8 in 1760, declined to 16.0 in 1769, and then ranged from 17.0 to 18.3 from 1770 to 1775.[7]

The counterpart of high and sustained consumer demand and rising prices in Europe was expanded production of tropical staples in the West Indies. Although most of the expansion occurred in the large island colonies of St Domingue and Jamaica, other islands

[5] John Campbell, *Candid and Impartial Considerations on the Nature of the Sugar Trade* (London, 1763), p. 31; David MacPherson, *Annals of Commerce*, (4 vols. Edinburgh, 1805), Vol. III, pp. 262, 583.

[6] Public Record Office, London, C.O. 388/24, R142; Edward Long, *The History of Jamaica*, (3 vols. London, 1774), Vol. I, pp. 519-21.

[7] David H. Makinson, *Barbados: A Study of North-American–West-Indian Relations 1739–1789* (The Hague, 1964), p. 34; Henri Hauser, *Recherchés et Documents sur l'Histoire des Prix en France de 1500 à 1800* (Paris, 1936), pp. 141-2.

and continental areas were caught up in the movement. Planters in the long-settled islands in the Lesser Antilles responded by increasing the size and productive capacity of their estates. Lacking virgin soils, they developed a system of husbandry requiring heavy application of labour and capital, or what may be termed a system of 'intensive-monoculture'.

A development of some importance was the opening of plantation frontiers in islands of the Lesser Antilles hitherto neglected because of international rivalry and/or the presence of hostile Indians. Included in the new areas of exploitation were the Danish islands of St John, St Thomas, and particularly St Croix; and the four 'neutral' islands which were ceded to Britain by the Treaty of Paris —Grenada, Tobago, St Vincent, and Dominica. Carving out new plantations in these and other islands were numerous Barbadians and Leeward Islanders, some of whom went further afield to the Dutch mainland colonies of Essequibo, Demerara, and Berbice.

II

The story is told of Edmund Burke, who, on the occasion of a social gathering at Sir Joshua Reynolds' house, spoke so convincingly of the fortunes to be made in the West Indies 'that Mrs. Horneck, a widow with two beautiful daughters, resolved to lose no time in purchasing where such advantages would infallibly arise. She did so, and lost a large portion of her slender income'. Burke's exaggerated opinion of the sugar colonies may be compared with the shrewd appraisal of an anonymous Jamaican:

> We would not be thought to speak with contempt of a West-India property. We think it has been proved, that with care and frugality, the planter's occupation will be very profitable. We mean only to shew, that the profits are not so enormous as many half-informed arithmeticians imagine. That, in fact, they are such as will yield a very comfortable maintenance to a proprietor who acts with constant circumspection and economy, and agreeable to the unerring counsel, which his annual state of accounts will present to his view.

In the Jamaican's view, it was dishonest to tempt new adventurers 'with exaggerated prospects of immoderate gain . . . '.[8]

---

[8] *Wraxall's Memoirs*, ed. Wheatley (London, 1884), Vol. II, n. 28; Anonymous review of *American Husbandry* in *The Monthly Review or Literary Journal* (London, 1776), Vol. LIV.

Permanent settlers commonly had little capital and began their planting careers with minor staples. James Knight, colonial agent for Jamaica, said that the general method was to begin with fifteen or twenty Negroes, who were first employed to clear a piece of land, build themselves houses, and plant provisions for their subsistence.

> The Planter then opens more land, and plants Ginger, Cotton, or some other commodity that is raised with a few hands; as he thrives, he purchases more Negroes, clears more land; and when he finds himself in a Condition, or able to attempt it by his Credit, and the Assistance of Friends, he then goes upon settling a Sugar-Work.[9]

Edward Long estimated that £1,000 sterling was necessary to begin an indigo plantation of 25 acres of land worked by 20 Negro slaves. Under skilful management such an estate would return £800 sterling per annum. On the other hand, his estimates of three newly-settled sugar plantations, ranging from 300 to 900 acres and from 39 to 300 slaves, were £3,515, £10,017, and £28,039—all in sterling money.[10]

Annual expenses amounted to a considerable sum of money on a large and fully settled plantation. One estimate concerns an Antigua estate of 500 acres and 300 Negroes, yielding annually 200 hogsheads of sugar and 120 puncheons of rum and valued at approximately £20,000 sterling. Average annual expenditures ran to £1,274; consisting of provisions £300; other supplies £290; salaries and wages £320; colonial and parish taxes £254; and crown duties and fees £110. The author failed to include the depreciation charges for slaves, which for an estate of 300 Negroes would have been about ten slaves at £40, or £400. Also omitted were enumeration duties of 1s 6d per hundredweight on sugar shipped to British North America, and duties of 6s 6d per hundredweight on sugar and 5s 3d per gallon on rum imported into Great Britain, or a total of about £220. After revising the estimate to include items originally omitted, total annual charges came to nearly £1,900 out of an annual gross revenue of approximately £3,600.[11]

'A sugar plantation is like a little town: it requires the produce, as well as the industry, of every climate', wrote William Beckford,

[9] James Knight, MS. *History of Jamaica*, Vol. II, Pt. 8, f. 141, British Museum *Additional* MS. 12,419.
[10] Long, *op. cit.*, Vol. I, p. 407.
[11] Anon., *Some Observations . . . of our New India Colonies* (London, 1764), pp. 48–51.

the Jamaica planter-historian.[12] A resident of Barbados emphasised the dependence of that island upon imported productive factors when he wrote to a friend in London that

> if the ships shou'd omitt coming from London and Bristoll we should go naked for want of cloths, if from Ireland we should be starved for want of Biefe and Butter, if from Pensilvania for want of Bread, if from New England the Sugar must Rot upon the Ground and the Rum and Molossus be thrown away for want of casks to put them in, if from the Maderas we shou'd faint for want of Wine, and if from Guinny the land would lye useless for want of slaves to cultivate the Ground, so that we are not able to Subsist either in victualls, drink or Clothes without assistance from forreign parts . . .[13]

Profitable staple production thus depended on uninterrupted supplies of productive factors at prices which were low in relation to those of final products. Practice fell short of theory, however, and it will be pertinent to enquire into the factors impeding and facilitating the supply of productive factors.

Once the productive factors were combined in a plantation unit, the proprietor had to contend with a host of risks and uncertainties before his crop was ready for market. These included wars, hurricanes, earthquakes, drought, floods, crop disease, slave and livestock mortality, slave absenteeism and insurrection, and pilferage and theft.

Then there were the risks and uncertainties attending the transportation and marketing of the staple commodities. Generally speaking, the small planter sold his produce to a local merchant or factor, while the individual possessing a large estate employed a commission agent in the metropolis to sell his staples, purchase supplies, and provide shipping, financial, and personal services. As one pamphleteer explained the problem, the planter

> is at a prodigious Distance from the Market, does not know what the Consumption may be, nor what Quantity of Sugar may be sent from the other Islands, and being already in Debt . . . he pays Ten or Eight per cent. per ann. Interest. He must be ruin'd if those [servants,

[12] William Beckford, *A Descriptive Account of the Island of Jamaica*, (2 vols. London, 1790), Vol. I, p. 141.

[13] 'T. Walduck's Letters from Barbados, 1710', *The Journal of the Barbados Museum and Historical Society*, Vol. xv, no. 1 (Nov. 1947), p. 35. For an excellent discussion of risk and uncertainty in the sugar industry, see Douglas G. Hall, 'Incalculability as a Feature of Sugar Production during the Eighteenth Century', *Social and Economic Studies*, Vol. x, no. 3 (Sept. 1961), pp. 340–52.

slaves, and cattle] are not kept employ'd, and he can have not other Way to employ them but in making Sugar, and makes as much as ever he can, and sends it to Market, upon distant Hopes that it will fetch a Price in proportion to the Expense and Trouble he hath been at, and when it is at Market he must sell it for what the Sugar Baker and Grocer will please to give him.[14]

Under favourable conditions the planters who employed commission agents absorbed the not inconsiderable profits of local middlemen. On the other hand, planters were out of their money for a lengthy period of time, and their costs included such variable items as freight, insurance, and duties.

III

Hazards there were, it is true, but they were often exaggerated by planters who sought special privileges from parliaments and crown officials. Actually, certain elements of risk and uncertainty were substantially reduced in the period of this study, notwithstanding the disruptive effects of the Seven Years' War. Productive factors were not only supplied in greater quantity, but they also became available from alternative sources with the expansion of overseas supply centres, the rise of free ports in certain West India islands, and the growth of informal empires. Similarly, the geographical spread of product markets in Europe and America gave the planters alternative outlets and made them less dependent on the vagaries of a single market. As more and more ships entered the plantation trade, it became feasible to adapt ship design to cargo requirements, to develop specialised branches of trade and shipping, and to reduce turnaround time in port. Though hazardous in wartime, merchant shipping was virtually freed from the menace of pirates and Spanish *Guarda-Costas* by the middle of the eighteenth century. No doubt the mercantile restrictions of metropolitan governments limited access to alternative markets and sources of supply, yet the evidence points to substantial improvement in factor and product markets, fewer impediments to resource allocation, and economies of scale— in sum, to improved economic organisation.

[14] Anon., *A Letter to a Member of Parliament Concerning the Importance of Our Sugar-Colonies to Great Britain* (London, 1745), p. 4.

If the colonies were grouped according to metropolitan affiliation, it is evident that they shared unequally in improved economic organisation. Britain and France, the great rivals of the age, varied in their ability to supply goods and services and absorb colonial staples. French planters had more territory adapted to tropical agriculture, advantages in recruiting white settlers, less burdensome taxes and duties, and more commercial privileges. British planters obtained slaves and North American supplies more cheaply, paid proportionately less for freight and insurance, had a better home market for sugar products, and received greater protection in wartime.

There is no doubt that Britain held the upper hand in wartime. During the Seven Years' War British military forces captured the islands of Guadeloupe and Martinique from the French, and the port of Havana from the Spaniards, only to give them back at the Peace of Paris. Owing chiefly to superior convoy service, few wartime losses were suffered in the trade between Britain and her sugar colonies. On the other hand, the British blockade almost destroyed the slave trade of Nantes and was disastrous for the West India trade of the leading port cities of France.

To superior seapower was added the advantage which British planters held over their rivals by their command of the protected home market. The home market expanded in breadth and depth, for the Act of Union in 1707 brought Scotland into the Empire, and acts of Parliament in the 1730s made Ireland a captive market for colonial goods. Since foreign sugar paid duties in Great Britain amounting to more than three times those levied on the colonial product, and smuggling was of limited scope, British planters had a home market that was superior to the foreign market. French planters likewise had a protected home market, but as the greater portion of their sugar was re-exported, the price at home was determined very largely by values realised from sales in re-export markets.[15]

Demand in the protected British market not only outpaced the productive capacity of the sugar colonies, but imbalances also became evident in the North American provision and lumber trades. The tendency for the North American colonies to grow more rapidly than their counterparts in the British Caribbean, together with the lag of the latter behind the foreign sugar colonies, supplied the basis

[15] Joseph Massie, *A State of the British Sugar-Colony Trade* (London, 1759), pp. 21–8.

for a thriving trade between the British Northern Colonies and the French and Dutch West Indies. The trade continued to grow despite the Molasses Act of 1773, which levied prohibitive duties on foreign sugar products imported into Britain's island and mainland colonies in America. Moreover, by retaining Canada and returning Guadeloupe and Martinique to France in 1763, the temperate-tropical imbalance of the British Empire was accentuated even further. Counteracting the imbalance after 1763, however, were such factors as the expansion of tropical agriculture in Jamaica, the planting of the ceded islands, and stricter enforcement of the Navigation Acts. 'The purchasing power of the Southern and West India colonists', writes Frank W. Pitman, 'was always limited in comparison with the enormous supply of Northern products. The empire was overbalanced on its temperate zone side. On the contrary, the French empire in the same period was overweighted on its tropical side'.[16]

Similarly, Britain's ability to supply African slaves increased in relation to the demand of her sugar colonies, whereaas the supply commonly fell short of the demand in the foreign sugar colonies. Leadership in the slave trade can be traced to the Asiento contract of 1713, whereby the South Sea Company of England was authorised to import 4,800 slaves annually into the Spanish Colonies. Loss of the Asiento in 1739 was more than compensated for by wartime expansion of supply centres and markets and the clandestine trade in slaves. During the Seven Years' War the British captured Goree and Senegal, the French West African slave trading posts at the same time that large numbers of slaves were introduced into Guadeloupe, Martinique, and Havana.[17]

After 1750, the merchants of Liverpool and Bristol commanded a growing portion of the traffic in human chattels. According to a commercial annalist, British and British American vessels carried from West Africa to the plantations and mines of America 59,400 out of a total of 97,120 Negro slaves in 1768. Of the remainder, 23,520 were carried by the French, 11,300 by the Dutch, 1,700 by the Portuguese, and 1,200 by the Danes. Lord Sheffield asserted in 1784 that the British had such a decided superiority over the French in the African trade, 'that it is allowed we have slaves one-

[16] Frank W. Pitman, *The Development of the British West Indies 1700–1763* (New Haven, 1917), pp. 189–90.
[17] Richard Pares, *War and Trade in the West Indies 1739–1763* (Oxford, 1936), pp. 188–91.

sixth cheaper'. A substantial portion of these slaves were re-exported to the foreign West Indies from Jamaica, Dominica, and Grenada.[18]

In the main, British planters jealously defended an imperial system which afforded them relatively cheap and plentiful supplies of factor inputs and a home market which expanded more rapidly than the supply base in the West Indies. A minority group of planters, on the other hand, sought to allay criticism of the West India monopoly by supporting policies of territorial and economic expansion. One warning note came from Samuel Martin, the leading planter of Antigua. Writing to his eldest son and namesake, the member of parliament, he declared in 1762 that 'if our Sugar Colonies are not extended in proportion to our African trade, and the extension of our North American settlements, the French Colonies will have all ye benefit of that extension, as it has even now, in time of war, the principal benefit of our North American trade at Hispaniola'.[19]

But the failure to heed Martin's warning was not the only reason for the more rapid expansion of the foreign sugar islands. The rapidity of settlement and astonishing increase of the French islands was attributed by Edward Long to 'the work of a wise policy, and a right turn their government has taken'. France spared 'neither useful expedients, nor money' in promoting her colonies, 'attending to their progress and welfare with a watchful eye, and unremitting diligence'. It was the contention of Lord Brougham that the superior productiveness of the soil of St Domingue enabled the planters 'to bring their sugar to market at a much lower price than the British, notwithstanding the additional expense, both in prime cost of the slaves, and in the freight of the commodities to Europe'. Compared with their British rivals, the French and other foreign planters lived more frugally and reinvested a larger portion of their profits in plantation expansion. In Lord Sheffield's opinion, the expensive manner in which the British planters lived could not be accomodated to small profit. French planters, by contrast, were said to resemble English yeomen and farmers in their manner of life.[20]

---

[18] MacPherson, *op cit.*, Vol. III, p. 484; John Lord Sheffield, *Observations on the Commerce of the American States*, new ed. (London, 1784), p. 160.

[19] *Letter Book of Samuel Martin*, 12 Feb. 1762, British Museum Additional MS. 41347, f. 122.

[20] Long, *op. cit.*, pp. 433–4; Henry Brougham, *An Inquiry into the Colonial Policy of the European Powers*, (2 vols. Edinburgh, 1803), Vol. II, pp. 520–1; Sheffield, *op. cit.*, p. 160.

IV

European possessions in the West Indies varied widely in area, resources, and level of economic and social development. Initially,
freemen and indentured servants worked the fresh soils of the smaller
islands and enjoyed a rude state of prosperity. Then came a period
of more careful cultivation, the consolidation of smallholdings into
plantations worked by Negro slaves, and high prosperity. Servants
out of their time found it increasingly difficult to purchase land and
become proprietors. They struck out for new frontiers, as did numerous planters who faced diminishing fertility and rising costs. New
settlements were occupied, new areas of production opened. Migrants
went near and far, to islands small and large, and to continental
colonies. Most found a new home under a familiar flag, but others
ventured on to foreign soil. Growing competition induced the planters in the older colonies to seek protective market arrangements
with the metropolitan governement. These measures, together with
capital, economy, and skill, made up in part for the lost advantages
of fertility and high yields.

Barbados was the first colony in the Lesser Antilles to achieve a
high plantation culture. After a 'golden age' in the 1650s and 1660s,
the islanders developed a near-monoculture sugar economy which
was conducted on a sustained yield basis. Natural disasters, together with wars and depressions, at times took a heavy toll of life
and property. Yet this tiny export economy, with its high dependence
on external markets and sources of productive factors, always managed to rise from the ashes of despair. Severe drought and depression
occurred in the 1680s and again in the 1730s. But by 1747, when
the governor made the following report, Barbados was well on the
road to recovery.

> The whole Island is cultivated by the Inhabitants in some manner or
> other, except such parts as are worn out and Impoverished, that the
> Labour of Manuring the same would not be recompensed, of wch Sort
> there are several thousand Acres, part whereof the Owners of the
> Sugar Work Plantations Use as Pasture for the large Quantitys of
> Cattle they are obliged to keep for the Manure even of their best
> Lands and for carrying their Effects to Markett.[21]

[21] Thomas Robinson to Board of Trade, 20 Feb. 1746/7, Public Records
Office, London, C.O. 28/57, Bb. 57.

Colony-wide statistics, together with the records of the Codrington plantations in Barbados, show that the long years of depression and limited recovery were followed by mild prosperity from 1748 to 1765 or 1770. Barbadian sugar exports to England rose from an annual average of 6,118 tons in 1731–5 to 6,993 in 1751–5, and to a high point of 9,069 in 1761–5. After a slight decline in 1766–70, exports fell to 5,634 in 1771–5.[22]

It should not be thought that the rise in staple exports resulted in a prosperity that was widely diffused. On the contrary, prosperity for the few was compatible with poverty for the many. During his visit to Barbados in 1751, George Washington was surprised to find that planters who possessed estates of two, three, and four hundred acres were in dire straits. 'How wonderful that such people shou'd be in debt', he exclaimed, 'and not be able to indulge themselves in all the Luxurys as well as necessarys of Life.' Apparently some planters escaped the debt trap, for the Virginian observed: 'There are a few who may be call'd midling people; they are either very rich or very poor, for by a Law of the Island Every Gent$^{n.}$ is oblig'd to keep a white person for ten Acres capable of acting in the Militia and consequently those persons so kept can't but be very poor'. George Frere, a local planter-historian, asserted that, owing to oppressive taxes, high costs, and mismanagement, 'the landed interest of Barbados (that is throughout the whole island) does not clear communibus annis four per Cent. estimating the principal at what land usually sells for'. The fact that the Codrington plantations cleared more than £2,000 a year on the average from 1753 to 1770 suggests that Frere's estimate may have been overly pessimistic.[23]

St Christopher, the first Caribbean island to be colonised by the English and French, was extolled in the eighteenth century as the 'garden of the West Indies'. This was due to its excellent volcanic soils, the salubrity of its climate, and the abundance of its harvests. After 1713, the island's sugar industry experienced a remarkable

[22] J. Harry Bennett, Jr., *Bondsmen and Bishops: Slavery and Apprenticeship on the Codrington Plantations in Barbados, 1710–1833* (Berkeley and Los Angeles, 1958), pp. 4–6; Noel Deerr, *The History of Sugar*, (2 vols. London, 1949–50), p. 193.

[23] John C. Fitzpatrick (ed.), *The Diaries of George Washington, 1748–1799* (New York, 1925), Vol. I, pp. 26–8; George Frere, *A Short History of Barbados* (London, 1767), pp. 105–7; Bennett, *op. cit.*, p. 6.

growth, particularly that portion of the island which was ceded by France to England.

Into the sugar frontier moved established planters and newcomers, of whom a number were Scottish. While the white population rose for a time and then declined to about 1,900 in 1775, Negro slaves far outstripped the whites, increasing from 3,258 in 1708 to 23,462 in 1775. Sugar exports to England increased more than elevenfold, rising from an annual average of 819 tons in 1706–10 to 9,143 tons in 1771–5. In the latter period the capital stock of this tiny island, which was divided among fewer than 120 proprietors, was appraised at £4 million, of which £1,300,000 consisted of Negro slaves. Moreover, according to a calculation of 1770, sugar made up £338,609 of total exports to the mother country of £367,074 sterling—all valued at current prices in the island.[24]

As with Barbados, St Christopher experienced a declining rate of growth after the boom years. 'There are Negroes yet wanting', wrote Governor Mathew in 1734, 'and the Island wants some farther Improvements. But this want of Negroes will arise rather from the Lands growing poorer, Consequently, more to be Tended and manur'd than from want of Strength to put more of it, than at present, in Culture'.[25] It was said that in order to maintain cane yields the proprietors had applied more manure to their lands in one year than was commonly applied to all the cane-lands of Jamaica in three. Cattle and mules were brought into pens or enclosures at night, where their dung was mixed with grass, decayed leaves, and offals of the sugar cane. James Ramsay described the average pen as 'perhaps of sixty by eighty feet, in which, from thirty to fifty cattle and mules are kept and fed'. In Ramsay's judgment, the peculiar fertility of St Christopher had the most baneful effects: 'It enables the greatest part of its proprietors to live in England; where, insensible of the sufferings of slaves, they think and dream of nothing but sugar, sugar; to which, in consequence, every spot of land is condemned'. A Scots lady was told during her visit to Antigua in 1774 that St Christopher had been 'almost abandoned to Overseers and

[24] John Campbell, *A Political Survey of Britain*, (2 vols. London, 1774), Vol. II, p. 671; Deerr, *op. cit.*, Vol. I, p. 197; James Ramsay, *A Reply to the Personal Invectives and Objections to An Essay on the Treatment and Conversion of African Slaves in the British Colonies* (London, 1785), p. 94.
[25] Gov. Mathew to Board of Trade, 31 Aug. 1734, Public Records Office, London, C.O. 152/20 V 46, f. 159.

managers, owing to the amazing fortunes that belong to Individuals, who almost all reside in England'.[26]

Antigua, the seat of government of the Leeward Islands and the largest island of the group, was described by two Scots visitors at the meridian of its prosperity. Lord Adam Gordan landed in Antigua in May of 1764. St John's, the principal town and seat of government, was said to be regularly laid out; 'the Court House, Council room, and Assembly room, are grand and well contrived ...'. From St John's he set out on a tour of the island, noting that 'almost all the people of fashion live on their Estates in the Country, and are all more or less engaged in making of Sugar and Rum'. For want of springs and rivers much effort had been expended in constructing cisterns and catch basins. The 'poor Negroes' were required to carry water on their heads to cool the stills used in the making of rum. 'Upon the whole it is a very happy Island', concluded Lord Gordon, 'the Society is good, and they have no disputes, but live all well together, in good harmony. I never met with more Civilities, during a Weeks stay, or left a place with more regret'.[27]

More varied were the impressions of Janet Schaw who visited Antigua in the winter of 1774-5. She found St John's 'very neat and pretty', consisting of sixteen streets which all lay to the trade winds in full view of the bay. The ladies were said to 'have the fashions every six weeks from London, and London itself cannot boast of more elegant shops than you meet with at St John's ...'. One of the most beautiful sights was the 'Negroes in joyful troops on the way to town with their Merchandize'—fruit, poultry, and vegetables—to sell at the weekly market.[28]

After a short stay in St John's, Miss Schaw visited the homes and plantations of friends in the country. From the high elevation of Dr John Dunbar's estate near St John's, she viewed the bay, the shipping, the town, and many rich plantations. 'Indeed it is almost impossible to conceive of so much beauty and riches under the eye in one moment. The fields all the way down to the town are divided

[26] James Ramsay, *An Essay on the Treatment and Conversion of African Slaves in the British Colonies* (London, 1784), pp. 74, 80, 118; Evangeline and Charles M. Andrews (eds.), *Journal of a Lady of Quality* (New Haven, 1921), p. 92.

[27] Lord Adam Gordon, 'Journal of an Officer in the West Indies, 1764 and 1765', *Travels in the American Colonies*, ed. Newton D. Mereness (New York, 1916), pp. 375-6.

[28] Andrews, *op. cit.*, pp. 87-8, 108, 115.

into cane pieces by hedges of different kinds'. She toured almost from one end of the island to the other, recording in some detail her impressions of the island and its people, and especially the planters who entertained her with lavish dinners and frequent balls. One early morning tour with a party of friends was described as 'a charming ride through many rich and noble plantations, several of which belonged to Scotch proprietors . . .'.[29]

Not all of Miss Schaw's observations were favourable. While the 'crack of the inhuman whip' was not heard during the Christmas season when the slaves enjoyed unbounded freedom, 'every man on the island is in arms and patrols go all round the different plantations as well as keep guard in the town'. Especially distasteful to the Scots lady were the 'licentious and even unnatural amours' of the white men, 'which appears too plainly from the crouds of Mallatoes . . .'. She noted the destructive effects of a recent hurricane, the incidence of droughts, and the turning of numerous plantations into grass to recover the strength they had lost by too many crops of sugar. After commenting on the ill effects of absenteeism, Miss Schaw observed that 'Antigua has more proprietors on it however than any of the other Islands, which gives it a great superiority'.[30]

Colonel Samuel Martin (1693–1776) was described by Miss Schaw as 'the most delightful character I have ever met with . . . the father of Antigua to whom it owes a thousand advantages, and whose age is yet daily employed to render it more improved and happy'. After living in England for a number of years, Martin returned to Antigua in 1750 to find his Greencastle plantation in a run-down condition. Embarking on an ambitious programme of reconstruction, he rebuilt his sugar works, added to his stock of slaves and livestock, and increased the yield of his cane-lands by means of innovations in tillage, drainage, and the application of fertilisers. In an appraisement of 1768, Greenfield contained 605 acres of land, 304 Negro slaves, together with buildings and equipment of a total estimated value of £32,000 sterling. In a letter of 20 March 1774, Martin wrote that the net produce of Greencastle 'for the last 3 bad Crops' amounted to £1,900 sterling per annum, or 5.13 per cent.[31]

[29] *Ibid.*, pp. 90–1, 100.
[30] *Ibid.*, pp. 91–2, 106, 112.
[31] *Ibid.*, pp. 103–4; Richard B. Sheridan, 'Samuel Martin, Innovating Sugar Planter of Antigua 1750–1776', *Agricultural History*, Vol. 34, no. 3 (1960), pp. 1–12.

Martin shared his knowledge with numerous young men who, after learning his rules of plantership, became managers and proprietors of plantations. Morevoer, he published an *Essay Upon Plantership*, which had run through five editions by 1773 and was described by a contemporary as 'an excellent performance, and to it I owe myself indebted'. John Campbell wrote in 1770 that the art of planting had been reduced to a regular system in Antigua and the neighbouring islands, 'and almost all the Defects of Soil so thoroughly removed by proper Management and Manure, that except for the Failure of Seasons, or the Want of Hands, there is seldom any Fear of a Crop'.[32]

Notwithstanding these improvements, the island's growth rate had slackened before Martin's death in 1776. The white population of Antigua declined from 5,200 to 2,590 between 1724 and 1774, while in the same period the slaves increased from 19,800 to 37,808. Sugar production increased under a system of near-monoculture, but not in proportion to the labour force. In fact, sugar exports to England increased from an annual average of 5,400 tons in 1721–5, to 7,745 in 1751–5, and to 7,923 in 1771–5. In 1768, Antigua had more than 300 sugar plantations, averaging about 200 acres and 100 slaves, each valued at £10,000 sterling. John Campbell estimated that Antigua's exports to Great Britain and Ireland in 1770 amounted to £359,243 sterling, of which £354,197 consisted of sugar and rum.[33]

V

The economic history of the Lesser Antilles falls into three parts in the years from 1748 to 1776. First came the years of peace from 1748 to 1756, then the Seven Years' War (1756–63), when the leading French islands were conquered and occupied by British forces, and, lastly, another interval of peace from 1763 to 1776. Under the terms of the Peace of Paris on 10 February 1763, Guadeloupe and Martinique were returned by Britain to France. Britain renounced all claim to the island of St Lucia, taking instead the islands of Dominica, St Vincent, Grenada, the Grenadines, and Tobago.

Martinique was in the most flourishing condition in the years pre-

---

[32] *Ibid.*, pp. 12–14; Campbell, *Political Survey of Britain*, Vol. II, p. 674.
[33] Deerr, *op. cit.*, Vol. I, p. 195; Anon, *Some Observations on Our New West India Colonies* (London, 1764), p. 50; Campbell, *op. cit.*, Vol. II, p. 673.

ceding the Seven Years' War. Sugar exports reached a peak of 20,544 tons in 1753, at which time the inhabitants consisted of 12,032 whites, 1,266 free mulattoes, and 64,827 Negro slaves. When the island fell to the English in August 1762, there were 116 water mills, each of which was reckoned to be worth two oxen or wind mills. After a short period of dislocation, the plantation economy revived under the encouragement of British and North American merchants, who supplied slaves, equipment, and provisions on generous credit. Furthermore, the planters were encouraged by the high prices that their produce commanded in British markets.[34]

If contemporary accounts are to be believed, Martinique suffered a series of reverses in the post-war period. These included the loss of part of the island's entrepôt trade, a destructive hurricane in August 1766, and a plague of ants which devastated part of the island, 'particularly the windward side, in such a manner, as to make it almost a desert, and ruined all the proprietors in that quarter'. On the other hand, the statistics compiled by Abbé Raynal point to substantial growth, although less marked than that of earlier years. Aggregate exports and re-exports, which amounted to £536,631 in 1769, had risen to £790,655 by 1775.[35] The census of 1770 returned 12,450 whites, 1,814 free mulattoes, and 70,553 slaves.[36]

Guadeloupe consists of two islands which are separated by a narrow channel. Basse-Terre, like Martinique, is high, rugged, and volcanic, while Grande-Terre is almost one continuous plain. In 1755, these two islands contained 9,643 whites, 41,140 slaves, 4,946 horse, 2,924 mules, and 13,716 horned cattle. Staples consisted of tobacco, indigo, cocoa, coffee, cotton, and particularly sugar, of which there were 334 plantations.[37]

After a siege of three months, when plantations were pillaged and some of the slaves carried off, Guadeloupe was conquered by the English in April, 1759. The English military governor reported that Basse-Terre contained 128 large sugar plantations, besides smaller ones for cotton and coffee, and was inhabited by 5,489 white men

[34] Deerr, *op. cit.*, Vol. I, p. 233; Guy Josa, *Les Industries du Sucre et du Rhum à la Martinique 1639–1931* (Paris, 1931), p. 97; Kate Hotblack, *Chatham's Colonial Policy* (London, 1917), pp. 66–7.
[35] Adam Anderson, *History of Commerce* (Dublin, 1790), Vol. V, pp. 304–5; Raynal, *op. cit.*, 1788 ed., Vol. VI, p. 91.
[36] Raynal, *op. cit.*, 1777 ed., Vol. IV, p. 166.
[37] *Ibid.*, p. 180.

and 16,298 Negroes. Grande-Terre had 190 sugar-works, the proprietors of which owned 17,566 able-bodied slaves.[38]

Submission to English rule was followed by a sudden transition
from misery to plenty. Having been virtually isolated by France's
inability to maintain communications in wartime, the islanders wel-
comed the English and North American traders who linked them
to external markets. Guadeloupe's prosperity during the four years
and three months of English occupation was based on 'cheap slaves
and necessaries, good prices, rapidly increasing cultivation, and new
creditors with clean slates'. Indeed, the English were reputed to have
stocked Guadeloupe with upwards of 18,000 slaves, and carried off
produce of an average annual value of £380,964 sterling.[39]

Unlike Martinique, Guadeloupe remained generally prosperous
after its return to France. As Abbé Raynal described the island's
advantages,

> It hath a greater number of slaves; it employs less of them in it's
> navigation and in it's commerce; it hath placed a number of them
> upon a soil which is inferior to that of its rival, but great part of which
> being newly manured, yields more abundant crops, than the grounds
> which are fatigued by a long continuance of tillage.[40]

However, the inhabitants were notorious for their clandestine
trade with neighbouring foreign islands, and largely for this reason
France gained less from Guadeloupe than she did from Martinique. In
1775, when Guadeloupe contained 13,000 whites, 85,000 slaves,
and 388 sugar plantations, the produce shipped to France amounted
to £531,292 sterling.[41]

VI

Closely associated with the Lesser Antilles by ties of trade and social
and economic organisation were the mainland colonies of France
and Holland in South America. Dutchmen, Frenchmen, and Englishmen had first settled 'the swampy no-man's-land' between Portuguese

[38] Hotblack, *op. cit.*, p. 59; Maurice Satineau, *Histoire de la Guadeloupe sous
l'Ancien Régime 1635-1789* (Paris, 1928), p. 211.
[39] Pares, *War and Trade*, pp. 188, 481, n. 3.
[40] Raynal, *op. cit.*, 1788 ed., Vol. VI, p. 113.
[41] *Idem.*

Brazil and Spanish Venezuela in the early seventeenth century. By the mid-eighteenth century slave-plantation colonies had been established in French Cayenne and Dutch Surinam, Essequibo, Demerara, and Berbice.

One of the great but little known tragedies after the Seven Years' War occurred in the underdeveloped colony of Cayenne. The Duc de Choiseul, the French chief minister, sought to compensate for the loss of Canada by planting an all-white colony on the mainland of South America to complement and support the sugar islands. Accordingly, some 14,000 emigrants were recruited by misleading propaganda and landed in Cayenne before the tropical wilderness was prepared for their reception. Famine and fever took such a heavy toll that within two years 11,000 colonists had died and 2,000 had returned to France. After this disastrous venture Cayenne became a slave-plantation colony; in 1788 it had 1,300 whites, 400 free Negroes, and 10,500 slaves.[42]

Surinam was the largest and most highly developed Dutch colony in the Guianas. By means of dikes, canals, wind mills and tide mills, the Dutch masters and their slaves watered coastal plains and river flood plains to secure abundant yields of tropical staples. In 1775, some 60,000 slaves, belonging to 2,823 masters, laboured on 430 large plantations. In the same year the produce of the colony was valued in Holland at £822,906 sterling, of which £347,225 consisted of sugar, £350,539 of coffee, £98,844 of cotton, £25,682 of cacao, and £616 of dye-woods. Though generally prosperous, Surinam was plagued by the flight of slaves to the back country where as many as 5,000 Maroons reputedly lived. Other difficulties included servile insurrection, a great coastal fire in 1770, a severe decline in coffee prices, and a financial crisis in Amsterdam in 1773 which ruined many debtor-planters. After 1773 a decline set in which was accentuated by the British conquest and occupation of Surinam during the Napoleonic Wars.[43]

The Dutch colony of Berbice on the river by the same name enjoyed a period of prosperity in the mid-eighteenth century before it was virtually destroyed by a series of calamities. In 1756, the white

[42] Herbert I. Priestley, *France Overseas Through the Old Régime* (New York, 1939), pp. 104–5; Deerr, *op. cit.*, Vol. II, p. 280.
[43] Radjnarain M. N. Panday, *Agriculture in Surinam 1650–1950* (Amsterdam, 1959), pp. 17–26; Deerr, *op. cit.*, Vol. I, p. 212; Raynal, *op. cit.*, 1788 ed., Vol. V, pp. 446–51.

people were attacked by an 'epidemical disorder' which lasted seven years. Greatly reduced in numbers, the whites were unable to control the 2,600 Negro slaves who laboured on 100 or more plantations. The slave revolt which began on 21 February 1763, spread rapidly until the entire colony was at the mercy of the rebels under the command of a Negro, Coffey. Indeed, some 200 of the 350 whites lost their lives before the rebels surrendered to Dutch and English military forces in March 1763.[44]

The fluctuating fortunes of Essequibo and Demerara were recorded in vivid detail by Laurens Storm Van's-Gravesande, Secretary and Bookkeeper to the Dutch West India Company from 1738 to 1772. After more than a century of settlement, Essequibo in 1762 had 68 plantations belonging to private planters and employing 2,571 slaves, and 3 plantations belonging to the West India Company. Seven years later there were 92 plantations with 3,986 slaves. Much more rapid was the growth of Demerara, which was first organised as a colony in 1746. At the end of 1768 the colony had 'thirty-four plantations more than in 1767', and in 1769 there were 206 plantations with 5,967 slaves.[45]

English planters from Barbados and the Leeward Islands played a prominant role in the development of Essequibo and Demerara. In the former colony there were seven English plantations by 2 October 1744, when Storm wrote:

> The English who have already established themselves here spare neither trouble, industry, nor cost, and most of the planters are already beginning to follow their example. Several who intend to settle here are still expected, for the grounds in Barbados and Antigoa are completely exhausted and expenses are much heavier there than here.[46]

After 1746 the tide of immigration turned to Demerara, where the number of English plantations had risen to 56 by 1769.[47]

Most prominent among the English planters were the two Gedney Clarkes (father and son) of Barbados. Described as 'a man of judgment and of large means', the elder Clarke had commenced, in

---

[44] Panday, *op. cit.*, pp. 27–30; Raynal, *op. cit.*, Vol. v, pp. 455–6.

[45] Storm Van's-Gravesande, *The Rise of British Guiana Compiled from his Despatches*, eds. C. A. Harris and J. A. J. DeVilliers, (2 vols. London, 1911), Vol. I, pp. 213–4; Vol. II, pp. 399–400. I am indebted to Mr. Richard Lobdell for bringing this source to my attention.

[46] *Ibid.*, Vol. I, p. 211.

[47] *Ibid.*, Vol. II, p. 400.

1752, 'the construction of a water-mill in Demerara, to be followed by two horse-mills, it being his intention to establish three plantations there'. One of the Clarke's plantations was said to have recouped the original investment of £12,000 sterling in a single year. When the Berbice rebellion threatened to engulf Demerara, the elder Clarke, in cooperation with the governor of Barbados, despatched five vessels with 200 English soldiers and equipment to save the Dutch colony. After the Berbice revolt Clarke became disenchanted with his eight plantation ventures in the Guianas. 'That gentleman is gradually getting rid of all his possessions, having now only two', wrote Storm on 21 February 1769. The two remaining properties had been sold by 15 May 1772.[48]

VII

Denmark was the fourth ranking north European power in the West Indies, holding the small islands of St John, St Thomas, and St Croix. St John and St Thomas each had 69 plantations in 1773, with a combined population of 6,620 slaves and only 446 white men. The somewhat larger island of St Croix was purchased by the Danish West India Company from France in 1733. A period of remarkable growth set in after 1754 when the Danish government purchased the privileges and effects of the Company and opened the colonial trade to all Danish subjects. Between 1753 and 1773 the slave population of St Croix increased from 7,566 to 22,244, while the island's sugar exports rose from about 320 to 8,230 tons.[49]

Lacking experienced planters, Negro slaves, and capital, Denmark made her colonies attractive to European investors and the planters of neighbouring foreign islands. Dutch loans to planters in the Danish West Indies amounted to more than £1 million sterling in 1773, while smaller amounts were claimed by Danes and Englishmen. After the demise of the West India Company, Englishmen came to dominate the slave trade to the Danish colonies. Experienced planters came from neighbouring Dutch and French colonies, and especially

[48] *Ibid.*, Vol. I, pp. 286, 390; Vol. II, pp. 599, 661.
[49] Waldemar Westergaard, *The Danish West Indies Under Company Rule, 1671–1754* (New York, 1917), pp. 222–49; Raynal, *op. cit.*, 1788 ed., Vol. V, pp. 486–9; Deerr, *op. cit.*, Vol. I, pp. 244–5.

from the English Leeward Islands. Already in 1741 there were about 300 Englishmen in St Croix 'who were none too amenable to Danish law or Company regulations'.[50]

Prominent among the British colonists of St Croix were Alexander Hamilton and Nicholas Tuite. While Hamilton's career is well documented, that of Tuite's is obscure. Tuite was born in Montserrat in 1705, of Irish extraction as were the majority of the colonists. In 1729 he owned 100 acres of land and 41 slaves in that island. He also engaged in a variety of trades, one of which was a sloop trade in slaves and Irish provisions to St Croix. After a hurricane ruined his property in Montserrat, he transferred his activities to St Croix. In 1776, he owned seven plantations there in his own right, and was part owner of seven others. He later became a West India merchant of Lime Street, London. After his death in 1772, a London newspaper said that Tuite had encouraged 700 English families to purchase estates in St Croix. On a visit to Copenhagen in 1760, he was 'acknowledged the founder of the colony, the sole source of its greatness and the finest character of the realm'. He was made Chamberlain to the King of Denmark. Tuite left an estate of £20,000 per annum to his only son, Nicholas Tuite Selby, who became a London banker.[51]

VIII

The four ceded islands, which were added to Britain's West India possessions at the close of the Seven Years' War, afforded an outlet within the Empire for the planters of the long-settled and crowded islands of the Lesser Antilles. Assisting the planters in the purchase of land and slaves were London-West India merchants and other British capitalists who invested heavily in the new colonies of Grenada, Tobago, St Vincent, and Dominica.

Grenada was the ceded island which experienced the most remarkable growth. It was described by a contemporary as 'full of large Mountains, forming several fertile Vallies, and producing a

---

[50] Raynal, *op. cit.*, Vol. v, p. 489; Westergaard, *op. cit.*, p. 222.

[51] See the biographical sketch of Nicholas Tuite in Philip C. Yorke (ed.), *The Diary of John Baker* (London, 1931), pp. 62–3. For Tuite's properties in St Croix, see Waldemar Westergaard, 'A St Croix Map of 1766: With a Note on its Significance in West Indian Plantation Economy', *The Journal of Negro History*, Vol. XXIII, no. 2 (April, 1938), pp. 216–28.

consisted of lands, buildings, equipment, livestock, and 284 slaves, of a total value of about 650,000 livres. The plantation was not un-encumbered, however, for debts were owing to mechants and other creditors to the amount of 299,000 livres. Records of receipts and expenditures for 1774 show that the plantation yielded a gross profit of 32 per cent, and probably a substantial net profit. On the other hand, the accounts for 1777–8 show a net loss of 5,409 livres. Be-sides the trade dislocations during the American Revolution, profits were curtailed by mismanagement, bad weather, slave and livestock mortality, and absentee's expenditures. In the end, the income from the estate was largely appropriated by the merchants and bankers of Poitiers and La Rochelle.[57]

Spanish possessions in the Greater Antilles—Cuba, Hispaniola, and Puerto Rico—lagged far behind those of France and Britain in economic development. Cuba made little progress as a plantation colony until the period following the Seven Years' War. The British conquest of Havana in 1762 marked a turning point, for, on the one hand, some 10,700 Negro slaves were introduced by British traders during the one year's occupation of the island, while, on the other hand, widespread reforms of the island's industry, trade, and military defence were launched by Charles III, the ablest of the Bourbon monarchs, to strengthen the colony against further attack. From the standpoint of the sugar industry, the chief 'reform' was the gradual abandonment of restrictions on slave imports by foreign traders. Under special licences, some 30,900 Negro slaves were introduced between 1763 and 1789, of which large numbers came from the British islands of Jamaica and Grenada. That these policies had some tangible effects is evident from the rise in the number of *ingenios,* or water mills, from 120 in 1765 to 473 in 1775, while sugar exports to Spain rose from 5,200 to 8,200 tons.

At a time when the British slave trade was coming under wide-spread attack and the French colony of St Domingue was nearing its holocaust, Cuba was rising to pre-eminence as a slave-plantation colony. In the course of a few decades the slow-paced hacendados were transformed into a driving, profit-seeking plantocracy. Alex-ander von Humboldt, an eye-witness of this transformation, said

[57] Gabriel Debien, 'Comptes, profits, esclaves et travaux de deux sucreries de Saint-Domingue (1774–1798)', *Revue de la Société d'Histoire et de Géographie d'Haiti*, Vol. 15, no. 55 (October, 1944), pp. 1–62.

that he had 'heard it coolly discussed, whether it were better for the proprietor not to subject the slaves to excessive labour, and consequently to replace them less frequently, or to draw all the advantage possible from them in a few years, and replace them oftener by the acquisition of bozal [imported] negroes'.[58]

X

Although smaller than Cuba and St Domingue, the island of Jamaica had nearly four times as much land as all the other British sugar islands put together. At mid-century it was estimated that the island contained 3.8 million acres: 1.7 million of mountainous and barren land, and 2.1 million capable of cultivation, of which only 0.5 million acres were actually occupied. There were approximately 12,000 whites, 130,000 Negro slaves, 455 sugar plantations, and probably a greater number of minor staple plantations, provision farms, and cattle pens. Though a variety of staples were cultivated, sugar made up nearly three-quarters of the value of the island's exports amounting to a little more than £1 million sterling.[59]

Jamaica was the subject of critical attention because the slow growth of its sugar industry was widely regarded as a primary cause of high sugar prices in England. The sugar refiners and grocers of London and Bristol petitioned Parliament in March 1753 for legislation to encourage sugar production in Jamaica, or to grant other relief. It was alleged that the proprietors of Jamaica 'though they have many hundred thousand Acres of Land fit for Sugar Plantations ... have notwithstanding forbore to cultivate them ... to the great Detriment of the Navigation and Revenue of this Kingdom, as well as of your Petitioners'. Owing largely to opposition from the powerful West India lobby, a bill for encouraging white settlement,

---

[58] Alexander von Humboldt, *Personal Narrative of Travels to the Equinoctial Regions of America*, tr. Thomasina Ross (3 vols. London, 1894), Vol. III, p. 244; Jacobo de la Pezuela, *Diccionario ... de la Isla de Cuba* (Madrid, 1863), Vol. I, p. 62; Hubert H. S. Aimes, *A History of Slavery in Cuba 1511 to 1868* (New York, 1907), pp. 32–51.

[59] Anon., *An Account of the Late Application to Parliament, From the Sugar Refiners, Grocers, etc. of London and Bristol* (London, 1753), p. 29; *Supra*, Table V, p. 41.

land reform, and the cultivation of lands then uncultivated in Jamaica was defeated in the House of Commons.[60]

Whatever the reasons for the slow expansion, and they are numerous and complex, the fact remains that Jamaica's plantation economy grew quite remarkably after the middle years of the century. From 1751 to 1775 a total of 835 slave ships brought 194,867 Negroes to Jamaica, of whom 27,569 were re-exported to other colonies. Thus a total of 167,298 slaves were retained, as compared with 123,944 in the 1726–50 period. The slave population was 205,261 in 1778 as compared with only 18,420 whites. Jamaica's sugar exports to Great Britain, which were produced on 775 plantations in 1774, more than doubled in the third quarter of the century. Minor staples also expanded. Edward Long wrote in 1774: 'Coffee was never cultivated to such heights as it is at present in Jamaica.' The CIF value of imports into Great Britain from Jamaica amounted to an annual average of £2,400,000 in the 1771–5 period, of which £1,750,000 consisted of sugar.[61]

Lord Adam Gordon was one of the numerous visitors who testified to the prosperity of the Jamaica gentry. After a voyage from Antigua, he landed at Port Royal on 18 June 1764. He toured most of the parishes, observing that the middle part of the island was very mountainous,

> tho' Interspersed with many fine Vallies, and feeding and breeding grounds—the Sugar Plantations are more frequent in the Lands that occupy seven or ten Miles of the Coast, and are extremely rich, altho' the expence of Stock, and Wear and Tear, is much greater than what attends any other kind of Estate, particularly when Negroes are at a high price.

Lord Gordon found the gentlemen of property 'extremely civil and remarkably hospitable to Strangers'. He visited many of their houses in the country and in Spanish Town, 'where they live elegantly and well, and are able to entertain their Guests in every respect better than people of the same property can do in Europe, particularly when one stays all night'.[62]

---

[60] *Ibid*, pp. 7–8, 25, 29; Anon., *A Short Account of the Interest and Conduct of The Jamaica Planters* (London, 1754), pp. 2–3, 16.
[61] Pitman, *op. cit.*, pp. 391–2; Long, *op. cit.*, Vol. I, p. 513; *Supra*, Table V, p. 41.
[62] Gordon, *op. cit.*, pp. 377–80.

Governor Trelawny commented on the remarkable expansion of Jamaica in the period from 1748 to 1770. In the former year the inhabitants had scarcely recovered from their fears of rebellious Negroes, and were unwilling to risk precarious settlements. In the latter year, on the other hand, the county of Cornwall in the west end of the island had improved so much as to make three-sevenths of the whole produce of the island. Moreover, the prosperity of the north side of the island was said to be 'much advanced by the great number of new plantations within ten miles of the sea, and by the increase of commerce at the free ports of Montego bay and Lucea'.[63]

Table I shows that the typical Jamaica sugar plantation was truly a big business unit in terms of acreage, labour force, industrial equipment, and capitalised value.

Table I

Estimate of a medium sized Sugar Plantation,
Jamaica, 1774
(Sterling Values)

	Number	Average Value	Total Value
Total Acres	600	£10 0s	£ 6,001
(Acres in Canes)	(266)	(16 1s)	(4,273)
Sugar Works			3,962
Negroes	204	37 6s	7,641
Livestock	174	7 19s	1,380
Utensils			340
Total			£19,324

SOURCE: Edward Long, *History of Jamaica* (1774), Vol. I, pp. 456–63; Jamaica Public Record Office, Spanish Town, *Inventorys*, Vol. 50, ff. 177–9.

Since there were 775 sugar plantations in 1774, the aggregate sugar property amounted to approximately £15 million. Other wealth, consisting of pens, small staple and provision farms, trading stocks, urban real estate, and non-sugar slaves and livestock, may be esti-

[63] MacPherson, *op. cit.*, Vol. III, p. 505.

mated at £3 million, thus making the total wealth of Jamaica some £18 million sterling.[64]

Estimates of the annual income and profit accruing to the Empire from the ownership of Jamaica are contained in the works of Edward Long and Bryan Edwards. Long's *Annual Profit of the Jamaica Trade to Great Britain* for the year 1773 has been checked against other sources and corrected where necessary by the writer. Similarly, the annual average 'neat proceeds' of the 775 sugar plantations for the years 1772–5, as shown in the Report of the Jamaica House of Assembly which is printed in Edwards' *History,* have been corrected and combined with Long's adjusted estimates in Table II.

Table II

Estimates of Annual Income and Profit Accruing to the Empire from the Ownership of the Colony of Jamaica, 1773
(Sterling Values)

	£	£
PROFITS ON TRADE		
Freight earnings	272,000	
Commission and brokerage	260,000	
Profit on manufacturing	116,650	
Slave trade	51,670	
Interest on loans	50,000	
Insurance	51,170	
Remittances to other areas	59,565	
Specie remittances	40,000	901,055
PROFITS ON RESIDENTIARY INDUSTRIES		
Urban rents, foodstuffs, etc.		111,300
PROFITS ON PRODUCTION FOR EXPORT		
Retained profits	334,700	
Remittances to Great Britain	200,000	534,700
TOTAL PROFIT FROM JAMAICA		£1,547,055

SOURCE: Edward Long, *History of Jamaica* (1774), Vol. I, p. 507; Bryan Edwards, *History of The British West Indies* (1793), Vol. II, pp. 463–7. Critical evaluation of Edward Long's profit estimates may be found in my 'The Wealth of Jamaica in the Eighteenth Century', *Econ. Hist. Rev.,* 2nd. ser. Vol. XVIII, no. 2 (August 1965), pp. 293–311; R. P. Thomas, 'The Sugar Colonies of the Old Empire: Profit or Loss for Great Britain ?' and my 'Rejoinder' to Thomas's article in *Econ. Hist. Rev.,* Vol. XXI, no. 1 (April 1968), pp. 30–45, 46–61.

[64] R. B. Sheridan, 'The Wealth of Jamaica in the Eighteenth Century', *The Economic History Review,* 2nd ser , Vol. XVIII, no. 2 (August 1965), pp. 292–303.

Profits of £1·55 million on a capital stock of £18 million gives an earning rate of 8·6 per cent, or a somewhat smaller return if allowance is made for the capital of merchants and manufacturers in the mother country. Even if such allowance is made, the return was probably well above the 4.5 per cent earned on real estate mortgages in England during this period, and much higher than the 3.5 per cent return on Consols.

XI

Although substantial profits accrued from the ownership of Jamaica as a whole, the shares going to different interest groups varied widely. As a percentage of total profits, trade accounted for 58.2; production for export 34·6; and residentiary industries 7·2. How much the rate of profit varied between economic groups is difficult to say, but one authority affirmed that the average rate of mercantile profit in England was 15 per cent. On the other hand, the profit accruing to the landed interest in Jamaica was probably not in excess of 5 per cent after payment of interest on debt and other charges. Edward Long calculated that a plantation valued at £14,000, if successfully conducted, yielded a profit of 10 per cent, which 'proves the ability of a planter to bear up under great debt for a considerable time; since, even paying 6 per cent per annum on the whole capital', he has still a reserve of 4 per cent for his own use, and casual expenditures'. While the large estates probably returned a comfortable margin to their owners, small planters and farmers were often hard pressed to make ends meet.[65]

Whether the wealthy planters were newcomers who parlayed income from trade, the professions, and other occupations in tropical agriculture, or members of old landed families, was a subject of speculation by contemporaries. It was Bryan Edwards' opinion that the fortunes in Jamaica were not the creation of a day, but the 'fruits of the toil of successive generations'. Edmund Burke, on the other hand, maintained that there were no parts of the world in which

[65] Phyllis Deane and W. A. Cole, *British Economic Growth 1688–1959* (Cambridge, 1962), p. 318; Long, *op cit.*, Vol. I, p. 461.

great estates were made in so short a time was the West Indies.[66]

Actually, both writers are correct insofar as the colonies of seventeenth century origin are concerned. Prominent among the mainstream families of Jamaica were those of Beckford, Long, Pennant, Bayly, Gales, Dawkins, Vassall, Ellis, Houghton, Lawrence, Barrett and Scarlett. The advantages and disadvantages of a head start are well illustrated by the experience of the Long family. Samuel Long, the founder of the family fortune, came out to Jamaica at the age of seventeen with the army of occupation. He acquired extensive properties, and became a leader of the colony as Chief Justice and member of the Council. During the two following generations the family estate was nearly lost by absentees' expenditures, mismanagement, and losses from speculation in the South Sea Bubble. Edward Long (1734–1813), the great grandson, was Speaker of the House of Assembly, Judge of the Vice-Admiralty Court, and historian of Jamaica. He resided on the island from 1756 to 1769, during which time he rebuilt the family fortune. His Lucky Valley plantation, which represented an investment of about £40,000, yielded an average net profit of 9.5 per cent during the years 1771–81.[67]

Though it dated from the foundation of the sugar colonies, absentee proprietorship among the mainstream families became a movement of consequence during the 'silver age'. Edward Long attributed the slow growth of the white population of Jamaica, in part, to

The emigration of many owners of property, who of late years have flocked to Britain and North America, beyond the example of former times, and drained those incomes from the island which formerly used to be spent there in subsisting various artificers, shop keepers, and other inhabitants . . .

Already in 1740, absenteeism was of sufficient scope to induce the legislators of Jamaica to pass a law requiring the agents and attornies of absentees and minors to submit annual reports of staple crops and their disposition to the local government. The 'Account Produce' volume for 1775 shows that 234 of the 775 sugar plantations were the property of absentees and minors. Similar reports of growing absenteeism are extant for the British colonies in

---

[66] Edwards, *op. cit.*, Vol. II, p. 456; William and Edmund Burke, *An Account of the European Settlements in America*, (2 vols. London, 1777), Vol. II, p. 104.
[67] British Museum Additional MS. 18,661, f. 80.

the Lesser Antilles, and for the French colony of St Domingue.[68]

Modern historians of the West Indies have emphasised the baneful effects of absentee proprietorship. Absenteeism contributed to the growing disproportion between whites and blacks, it tended to promote a careless, cruel, and extravagant management of plantations, it established conditions that led to slave insurrections, and it drained away wealth and income that might otherwise have gone into public and private improvements. Moreover, by depriving the colonies of men of talent, property, and experience, absenteeism contributed to the impoverishment of political and social life, at the same time that there grew up a West India aristocracy of wealth and political power which had a corrupting influence on the mother country.[69]

Absenteeism varied in extent and nature, however, and broad generalisations about its consequences are likely to be indefensible. As Professor Hall points out, the absentees were a heterogeneous lot:

> some were West Indian born, others had made their first appearance elsewhere; some had lived on their estates, others had never done so; some were completely ignorant of the details of sugar-making and the sugar trade, whereas others had practical experience of both; some were genteel, others were not.

In the light of their diverse character, it cannot be argued that absentees were necessarily superior to local inhabitants in matters of government and social leadership, or in managerial ability. Hall contends that 'the colonial elites were deprived of significant membership as much by internal social and demographic factors as by absenteeism'. Moreover, it cannot be contended that absentees were altogether parasitical, since numbers of them invested colonial wealth in West India trading houses, shipping, insurance, and industrial concerns, or represented the interest of the colonies in the mother parliament. Finally, Hall asserts: 'It is probably true that with or without absentee-ownership, wealth would have been drained from the colonies to Britain. The expectation of such a drain was

---

[68] Long, *op. cit.*, Vol. I, p. 386; *The Laws of Jamaica*, (2 vols. Jamaica, 1792), Vol. I, pp. 278–9; J.P.R.O., 'Spanish Town', *Account Produce*, Vol. VI; Pierre de Vaissière, *Saint-Domingue: La Société et la Vie Créoles sous l'Ancien Régime 1629–1789* (Paris, 1909), pp. 297–300.

[69] Lowell J. Ragatz, *The Fall of the Planter Class in the British Caribbean, 1763–1833* (New York, 1963), pp. 44–59; Eric Williams, *Capitalism and Slavery* (Chapel Hill, 1944), pp. 85–93; Pitman, *op. cit.*, pp. 13, 30–52.

one of the motives for the acquisition of 'tropical plantations'.[70]

As the 'saturated planters' returned to the mother country to enjoy their slave-produced wealth, 'planters-on-the-make' found their opportunities enhanced. From the ranks of trade, public administration, the professions, and plantation overseers and managers came a motley group to seek their fortunes in the sugar lottery. A Barbadian planter wrote that 'the Bulk of them, who come here to prey upon us, are either of the Learned Professions, or are Merchants ... the Lawyers thrive by our Contentions, the Physicians by our Diseases, and the Clergy live by the Sins of the People'. Not all of the planters-on-the-make were men. Governor Lawes said that the female way to become wealthy in a short time in Jamaica was summed up in two words, 'marry and bury'.[71]

Prominent among the newcomers were the Scotsmen whose ranks included governors, customs collectors, doctors, merchants, artisans, book-keepers, and overseers. Lower managerial positions on estates were commonly filled by young men from Scotland and Ireland. John Luffman observed that the overseers in Antigua were 'generally poor Scotch lads, who, by their assiduity and industry, frequently become masters of the plantations, to which they came out as indentured servants'. Scotsman with professional and mercantile qualifications generally made a speedier entry into the plantocracy. In Jamaica, the Scotsmen were described as in general 'sober, frugal, and civil; the good education, which the poorest of them receive, having great influence on their morals and behaviour'.

Jamaica, indeed, is greatly indebted to North-Britain, as very near one third of the inhabitants are either natives of that country, or descendants from those who were. Many have come from the same quarter every year, less in quest of fame, than of fortunes; and such is their industry and address, that few of them have been disappointed in their aim.

From the writer's studies of Scottish enterprise in Antigua, St Christopher, the ceded islands, and Jamaica, it seems evident that

[70] Douglas Hall, 'Absentee-Proprietorship in the British West Indies, To About 1850', *The Jamaican Historical Review*, Vol. IV (1964), pp. 15–35.

[71] Anon., *Caribbeana, Containing Letters and Dissertations, etc.*, (2 vols. London, 1741), Vol. I, p. 61; Long, *op. cit.*, Vol. II, p. 285.

the stereotyped image of the planter as an improvident, indolent, and sensuous gentleman stands in need of revision.[72]

Not a few Scotsmen went home to live on the income from their plantations. From Antigua Dr Walter Tullideph wrote to Alexander Campbell in Jamaica on 27 August 1746, congratulating him for being able to retire to Scotland and lay out his money on an agreeable residence for his family. Tullideph himself retired to Scotland a few years later after acquiring a fortune in Antigua as a doctor, merchant, and planter. Conspicuous among the absentees of St Christopher was William McDowall who established a large West India trading house in Glasgow and represented a Scottish borough in Parliament. Numerous West Indians purchased forfeited estates after the Stuart rising in 1745.[73]

XII

Absentee remittances, together with commissions, freight, insurance, and other 'invisibles', absorbed the greater part of the income of the West Indies. According to Abbé Raynal, imports into Europe from the West Indies in 1775 amounted to 261 million livres (or £10.9 million sterling), of which £0.3 million went to Denmark, £0.6 to Spain, £1.3 to Holland, £3.4 to England, and £5.3 to France.

> The labours of the people settled in those islands, are the sole basis of the African trade: they extend the fisheries and the cultures of North America, afford a good market for the manufactures of Asia, and double, perhaps treble, the activity of all Europe. They may be considered as the principal cause of the rapid motion which now agitates the universe.[74]

Though figures are lacking for other colonies, Table 11 suggests that 65 per cent or more of the annual income and profit of Jamaica went to residents of Great Britain and Ireland, of which 11.8 per cent consisted of absentee remittances.

[72] John Luffman, *A Brief Account of the Island of Antigua* (London, 1789), pp. 99–100; Long, *op. cit.*, Vol. II, pp. 286–7; R. B. Sheridan, 'The Rise of a Colonial Gentry: A Case Study of Antigua, 1730–1775', *The Economic History Review*, 2nd ser., Vol. XIII, no. 3 (1961), pp. 342–57.

[73] MS. *Letter Book of Dr. Walter Tullideph*; Gerrit P. Judd, *Members of Parliament, 1734–1832* (New Haven, 1955), pp. 265.

[74] Raynal, *op. cit.*, 1788 ed., Vol. VI, pp. 412–14.

Individually and collectively, the great fortunes accrued chiefly to the London-West India merchants, most of whom were members of prominent planter families and absentee proprietors in their own right. These were the men who became members of parliament, aldermen, lord mayors, baronets, and, in several instances, peers of the realm. Together with absentee planters and colonial agents, they advised ministers in the appointment of colonial governors, attorney generals, custom collectors, members of colonial councils, as well as looking after legislative matters affecting the colonies. They linked the plantations with the London product and money markets, shrewdly combining commission agencies with individual trading ventures, shipping, insurance, finance, and government contracts. At least seventy absentees sat in the House of Commons between 1730 and 1775. Numbered among the absentees from Antigua were twenty London-West India merchants, twelve members of parliament, one lord mayor of London, and nine titled persons.[75]

It should not be thought that much capital was drawn out of Europe to finance, govern, and defend the West India colonies. On the contrary, the profits of the plantations were the source which fed the indebtedness charged upon the plantations themselves. Not only were the West Indies largely self-financing after the initial investment in the seventeenth century, but also much of the wealth of the colonies eventually found a permanent home in Europe.[76]

Nor should it be thought that the dazzling fortunes of the few and the moderate fortunes of the many were gained without burdensome social costs. Private affluence for the oligarchy coexisted with both private and public poverty for the poor whites and Negro slaves. Judged by European standards of the time, the West Indies were notoriously deficient in education, social services, and public improvements. While the poor whites and free coloureds shouldered some of these costs, the greatest burden fell on the Negro slaves. Sugar production was more demanding of hard physical labour and more destructive to life and limb than that of most other tropical and semi-tropical staples. Contributing to the precarious and troubled life of the slaves were such factors as disease, accidents,

---

[75] Sheridan, 'Rise of a Colonial Gentry', p. 346; Lillian M. Penson, 'The London West India Interest in the Eighteenth Century', *The English Historical Review*, Vol. 36 (1921), pp. 373–92.
[76] Pares, 'Merchants and Planters', p. 50.

wars, natural disasters, dependence on imported foodstuffs, planter indebtedness, absenteeism, onerous slave codes, and cruel and capricious masters. Treatment varied, of course, from plantation to plantation, from colony to colony, as well as between the colonial systems of European nations. Professor Tannenbaum has ranked the three slave systems—north European, French, and Iberian—in order of severity and concludes that Dutch slavery was probably the harshest, that of Portugal the mildest, while the French system occupied a middle-ground position.[77]

Paradoxically, British colonial slavery was apparently harsher in the era of prosperity than it was in the subsequent period when secular decline was punctuated by wars, destructive hurricanes, and the short-lived prosperity of the 1790s. Of crucial importance in any discussion of slave welfare is the question of longevity and the capacity of the slave population to replace itself by natural increase. John Newton, the master of slave ships who later became a clergyman and anti-slavery leader, was told by a planter of Antigua that it was more economical

> to wear them [slaves] out before they became useless, and unable to do service; and then to buy new ones, to fill up their places [than] to appoint them moderate work, plenty of provision, and such treatment as might enable them to protract their lives to old age.

The planter went on to say 'he could mention several estates, in the island of Antigua, on which it was seldom known that a slave had lived above nine years'. Samuel Martin, on the other hand, maintained his labour force without any new purchases for some years prior to 1776.[78]

Evidence of milder slave treatment and less dependence on imports for replacement after about 1770 is extant for the islands of Barbados, Antigua, Nevis, Montserrat, and Jamaica.[79] To single out

---

[77] J. H. Parry and P. M. Sherlock, *A Short History of The West Indies* (London 1957), pp. 245–51; Frank Tannenbaum, *Slave and Citizen: The Negro in the Americas* (New York, 1963), p. 65, n. 153.

[78] John Newton, *The Journal of a Slave Trader 1750–1754*, eds. Bernard Martin and Mark Spurrell (London, 1962), p. 112; Andrews, *op. cit.*, p. 104.

[79] Bennett, *op. cit.*, pp. 44–74; James Stephen, *The Slavery of the British West India Colonies Delineated*, (2 vols. London, 1824), Vol. I, pp. 468–9; Richard Pares, *A West India Fortune* (London, 1950), pp. 121–32; Elsa Goveia, *Slave Society in the British Leeward Islands at the End of the Eighteenth Century* (New Haven, 1965), pp. 122–5; George W. Roberts, *The Population of Jamaica* (Cambridge, 1957), pp. 234–7.

the island of Jamaica for brief commentary, Hector M'Neill, on his second visit to the West Indies in 1787, observed a 'wonderful change for the better' in the treatment of slaves within a twenty-year period. No one denied, however, that 'the *Negroes* in this island are in *general* over-worked and under-fed, even on the mildest and best regulated properties'. He said that one of the greatest barriers to the propagation of slaves was the common practice of purchasing a greater number of males than females.[80]

There were several reasons advanced for the milder treatment of Negro slaves. The major reason, according to M'Neill, was the rise in slave prices which led the proprietors 'to view Negro Property as an object of great concern and consequently to preserve it by every prudent method'. Other writers pointed to natural and man-made disasters which induced planters to concern themselves with dietary, medical, breeding, and labour improvements. Indeed, the years from 1772 to 1783 witnessed a series of disasters, starting in 1772 with a destructive hurricane in the Leeward Islands, the credit crisis of the same year which led to widespread financial distress in the West Indies, the American Revolution which interrupted supplies of foodstuffs from North America, and, finally, the violent hurricanes which struck Jamaica in the 1780s and were in large measure responsible for the death of some 15,000 Negroes.[81]

Beginning chiefly in the era of prosperity, missionary endeavours in the West Indies and anti-slavery activity in Europe contributed materially to slave amelioration and eventual emancipation. In the vanguard were the Moravian Brethren from Germany who began their missionary enterprise in the Danish island of St John in 1732. Moravian missionaries came to Jamaica in 1754, to Antigua in 1756, and to Barbados in 1765. Except for the Danish islands and Antigua, they met with widespread opposition from the planters and made few converts among the slaves. Hostility was by no means negligible in Antigua, but it is interesting that some of the planters assumed personal responsibility for converting and baptising their slaves.

---

[80] Hector M'Neill, *Observations on the Treatment of Negroes, in the Island of Jamaica* (London, 1788), pp. 2–4, 44.

[81] *Ibid.*, p. 4; MacPherson, *op. cit.*, Vol. III, p. 526; Richard B. Sheridan, 'The British Credit Crisis of 1772 and The American Colonies', *The Journal of Economic History*, Vol XX, no. 2 (June 1960), pp. 164–73; Beckford, *op cit.*, Vol. I, pp. 89, 129–30; Vol. II, pp. 311–12.

This was the case with Samuel Martin and Nathaniel Gilbert. Gilbert was a leading planter and Speaker of the House of Assembly. During a visit to England he was brought into personal contact with John Wesley and became a Methodist. He returned to Antigua in 1760 and began to preach the gospel to his slaves. He founded a Methodist Society in the island which survived his death in 1774.[82]

Planters who returned to Europe discovered to their dismay that Enlightenment leaders were exerting a growing influence on public opinion, and indirectly on colonial policy. The Frenchman, Bernardin de St Pierre, said that he did not know whether coffee and sugar were necessary for the happiness of Europe, but he did know 'that these two articles had caused the unhappiness of two parts of the world. We have depopulated America in order to get a land to grow them; we have depopulated Africa in order to get a people to cultivate them'. Words were joined with action in 1772 when Chief Justice Mansfield handed down his famous decision which gave liberty to any slave brought to England, thereby setting free some 14,000 persons. Fifty one years were to elapse before this fateful decision was extended to the British colonies.[83]

XIII

The chapter of West India history delineated by this essay was almost an unqualified success story as viewed by European men of affairs. More colonial staples were sold in Europe, more European goods were sold in the colonies, more slaves and provisions were needed for the plantations, thus requiring more European goods with which to buy slaves and provisions. The whole was greater than the sum of its parts, for general business was greatly stimulated as well as capital accumulated. The dark side of the story waa one of forced prices, forced labour, rapid fortunes, rapid bankruptcies, high mortality, political corruption, conspicuous consumption amidst abject poverty, imperial rivalry, and international warfare. However, before

[82] Alfred Caldecott, *The Church in the West Indies* (London, 1898), pp. 72–6; Edwards, *op. cit.*, Vol. I, pp. 431–7.
[83] 'Voyage à l'île de France', *Oeuvres complètes de Jacques Henri Bernardin de Saint-Pierre*, ed. L. Aimé-Martin, (12 vols. Paris, 1818), Vol. I, pp. 152–63; T. B. Howell, *A Complete Collection of State Trials*, (34 vols. London, 1814), Vol. xx, pp. 70–82.

the debits had come to outweigh the credits on the balance sheet of empire, one country had captured a large enough segment of the Atlantic trading area to launch the Industrial Revolution. In the words of Dr Eric Williams, 'The commercial capitalism of the eighteenth century developed the wealth of Europe by means of slavery and monopoly. But in so doing it helped create the industrial capitalism of the nineteenth century, which turned round and destroyed the power of commercial capitalism, slavery, and all its works'.[84]

[84] Williams, *Capitalism and Slavery*, p. 210.

Gordon, Lord Adam, 86, 99
Goree, 81
Goveia, Elsa V., 40
Grapes, 40
Greater Antilles, 16, 38, 68, 97
Greencastle plantation, Antigua, 87
Grenada, 76, 82, 88, 94–5, 97; sugar production, 23
Grenadines, the, 88
Guadeloupe, 15, 16, 17, 80, 81, 88, 89–90; sugar production, 23
Guianas, 10, 15, 17, 26, 90–3
Guinea grass, 44

Haciendas, 61–6
Hacket, Sir Richard, 31
Hall, Douglas G., 104
Hamilton, Alexander, 94
Hamilton, Earl J., 63
Harrison family, Barbados, 31
Hauser, Henri, 24
Havana, 69, 80, 81, 97
Havana Company, 68
Henley estate, Barbados, 32
Henry the Navigator, 15
Hide hunters, 39; hides and tallow exported, 40, 62
Hispaniola, 15, 16, 39, 62; Spanish Hispaniola, *see* Santo Domingo
Holder family, Barbados, 31
Holland, *see* Dutch
Houghton family, Jamaica, 103
Hughes, Griffith, 31
Humboldt, A. von, 97
Husband, Sir Samuel, 31
Hussey, Roland D., 68

Indentured servants, 19, 27, 42, 83
Indians, 14, 26, 62, 63, 64, 65, 66, 69, 76; *see also* Carib Indians; Mosquito Indians
Indigo, 12, 14, 33, 40, 48, 50, 56, 66, 74, 77, 95, 96
Ireland, 78, 80
Irish, in Montserrat, 94; in West Indies, 105

Irrigation works, 51–3

Jamaica, 15, 16, 17, 56, 75, 77; sugar production, 23, 101; Spanish in, 39, 40, 62; British conquest, 39, 40; economy, 40–7, 48, 50, 52, 98–102; population, 42, 99, 103; Record Office, 46; slave trade, 82, 97; planters, 102–3; Scots, 105; slavery, 109
Jenkins' Ear, War of, 67
Jesuits, 48
Jews, 15, 16, 26

Kingston, Jamaica, 45, 67
Knight, James, 77

Labat, Père, 30, 37, 50
Land tenure, 31, 37, 44
Langford family, Antigua, 59
La Rochelle, 97
Law, John, 24
Lawes, Nicholas, 105
Lawrence family, Jamaica, 103
Le Cap (Cap François), 50, 96
Leeward Islands, 76, 86, 92, 109
Lesser Antilles, 11, 12, 15, 25, 39, 76, 88, 94, 103
Leybourne, William, 95
Ligon, Richard, 11
Lisbon, 67
Littleton, Edward, 28
Liverpool, 81
Livestock, 18, 30, 31, 40, 42, 43–4, 52, 85
Logwood, 39
London: West India merchants of, 27, 94, 107; sugar refiners, 98
Long, Edward, 17, 44, 45, 75, 77, 82, 99, 101, 102, 103
Long family, Jamaica, 103
Long, Samuel, 103
Louis XIV, 10
Lucea, Jamaica, 100
Lucky Valley plantation, Jamaica, 103
Luffman, John, 105

McDowall, William, 106
M'Neill, Hector, 43, 109
Madeira, 15, 78
Mahogany, 47
Malouet, Pierre Victor, 55
Malthus, Thomas R., 21
Mansfield, 1st Earl, Chief Justice, 110
Maroons, 39, 40, 91; Maroon War in Jamaica, 42, 45
Martin, Samuel, 57, 82, 87, 88, 108, 110
Martinique, 10, 15, 16, 17, 48, 50, 80, 81, 88; sugar production, 23; economy, 32–8, 89; population, 34, 89; slavery, 36, 38
Mathew, William, 85
Mercantile system, 9, 24, 59–61
Methodists, 110
Mexico, 62, 63, 64, 65, 66
Mines, gold and silver, 62, 63, 64, 65, 69
Mintz, Sidney W., 12
Missionaries, 109
Modyford, Sir Thomas, 40
Molasses Act, 81
Montego Bay, Jamaica, 100
Montserrat, 94, 108
Moravian missionaries, 109
Moreau de St Méry, M.L.E., 52, 53
Morgan, Sir Henry, 40
Mosquito Indians, 40

Nantes, 80
Navigation Acts, 24, 81
Negro artisans, 19, 37, 56–7
Nevis, 39, 108
New England, 78
Newton, A. P., 11
Newton, John, 108
Nonconformist families of Antigua, 59
North America, 10, 13, 24, 60; trade with West Indies, 18, 20, 32, 36, 47, 80–1, 82, 89, 90, 106, 109

Old Harbour, Jamaica, 45
Oldmixon, John, 31
Ortiz, Fernando, 18

Osborne family, Barbados, 31

Pares, Richard, 14, 18, 21, 74
Paris, Peace of, 76, 80, 88
Parliament, British: West India lobby at, 98; absentees in, 107
Pennant family, Jamaica, 103
Pennsylvania, 78
Peonage, 65
Pimento, 44, 47
Pinnock, Philip, 45
Pitman, F. W., 45, 81
Pitt, William, the elder, 67
Plantation colonies: and the mercantile system, 9–11, 24, 59–61, 67; economy, 12–14, 19–21, 55–8, 70, 77–9; British and French compared, 24–5, 80–2; Spanish, 61–6; see also Sugar plantations
Planters' social origins, 58–9, 102, 105
Plants, indigenous West Indian, 14
Poitiers, 96, 97
Port-au-Prince, St Domingue, 50
Port Royal, Jamaica, 40, 45
Portuguese: Jews, 15, 16, 26; colonies, sugar production in, 22; slave trade, 81; slave system, 108
Powell, Henry, 26n.
Priestley, Herbert I., 67
Puerto Rico, 23, 62, 69, 97

Ramsay, James, 57, 85
Raynal, Abbé, 38, 52, 74, 89, 90, 96, 106
Repartimiento system, 62, 63, 65
Rice, 15, 24
Roberts, G. W., 43
Robinson, Thomas, 83
Roucou, 33
Rum, 31, 37, 47, 75; duties, 77

St Andrew parish, Jamaica, 45
St Christopher, see St Kitts
St Croix, 76, 93, 94; sugar production, 23
St Domingue, 16, 17, 25, 39, 40, 75, 104; sugar production, 23; economy,

47–56, 82, 95–7; slavery, 50, 54–5;
irrigation works, 51–3
St George, Grenada, 95
St John, Virgin Islands, 76, 93, 109
St John's, Antigua, 86
St Kitts, 12, 33, 39, 58, 105, 106;
sugar production, 23; economy,
84–5
St Lucia, 88
St Pierre, Bernardin de, 110
St Thomas, Virgin Islands, 76, 93
St Vincent, 76, 88, 94
Santiago de Cuba, 69
Santo Domingo (Spanish Hispaniola),
52, 55, 69, 97
Sauer, Carl O., 15
Say, Jean Baptiste, 96
Scarlett family, Jamaica, 103
Schaw, Janet, 86, 87
Scotland, 80
Scots, 59, 85, 95, 105–6
Scott, John, 27
Selby, Nicholas Tuite, 94
Senegal, 81
Seven Years' War, 67, 79, 80, 81, 88,
91, 97
Sheffield, Lord John, 81, 82
Silver, 62, 63; bullion trade, 61, 67
Slave trade, 20, 21, 25, 62, 67, 73, 80,
81–2, 97
Slaves and slavery, 13, 19–21, 70, 73,
107–11; mortality, 21, 30, 43, 54–5,
108, 109; subsistence of slaves, 36,
43; insurrections, 40, 92, 93
   Slaves in Antigua, 108; Barbados,
27, 28, 29, 30, 108; British colonies,
108–9, 110; Cuba, 69, 97–8; Dutch
colonies, 108; French colonies, 25,
108; Jamaica, 42–3, 46, 109;
Martinique, 36, 38; Mexico, 66;
Portuguese colonies, 108; St
Domingue, 50, 54–5; St Kitts, 85;
Spanish colonies, 65, 66
Smith, Adam, 74
Sober, John, 31
South Carolina, 15
South Sea Company, 81

Spain: the Spanish, 10, 11, 60, 63, 67;
introduce sugar cane, 15; alliance
with France, 68; trading companies,
68; imports from West Indies, 106
Spanish colonies: attacks on, 10, 11,
39; export livestock, 18; sugar production, 22; economy, 61–9; trade
with British and French, 61, 67, 81;
society in, 61–2; slavery, 65, 66
Spanish Succession, War of, 68
Spanish Town, Jamaica, 99
Speciale, Pietro, 16
Storm Van'S-Gravesande, L., 92, 93
Sugar: cane imported to the New
World, 15; manufacture, 16–18, 31;
clayed sugar, 31, 34, 37, 47; refineries, 34; consumption in Britain and
France, 74–5; duties, 77, 80;
markets, 78, 79, 80, 83
Sugar plantations: operation of, 13,
56–8; location of, 14
Sugar production: transferred from
Brazil, 15–16; statistics of, 22–3;
combined industry and agriculture,
56; severity of labour in, 107; in
Antigua, 88; Barbados, 46–7, 83–4;
Cuba, 69; Hispaniola, 62; Jamaica,
45–7, 98–102; Martinique, 33–5,
37–8, 89; Mexico, 66; St Domingue,
48–54, 96–7; St Kitts, 84–5
Surinam, 15, 16, 58, 73; sugar production, 22; Maroons, 40n., 91;
economy, 91

Tannenbaum, Frank, 108
Thirty Years' War, 11, 60
Tobacco, 12, 14, 15, 24, 33, 36, 40, 48,
56, 68, 69
Tobago, 76, 88, 94
Tortuga, 39, 40
Toussaint L'Ouverture, 55
Trelawny, Sir William, 100
Trezel, Dutch merchant, 33
Tuite, Nicholas, 94
Tullidelph, Walter, 106

Utrecht, Treaty of, 18

Vassall family, Jamaica, 103
Venezuela, 68
Voltaire, *Candide*, 73

Wakefield, Edward Gibbon, 19
Walduck, T., 78n.
Walker family, Barbados, 31

Washington, George, 30, 38, 84
West India lobby, 98
White: servants and labourers, 19, 42;
    artisans, 37, 56; poor whites, 84, 107
Williams, Eric, 19, 111
Willoughby, William, Lord, 27
Winthrop family, Antigua, 59

Young, Arthur, 10

PROPOSED CONTENTS
A HISTORY OF THE WEST INDIES IN 3 VOLUMES

Vol. 1   The development of European empires in the West Indies to 1689

General introduction to the History

Chapters

1   The pre-history of the Caribbean
2   The Amerindian cultures of the West Indies
3   The voyages of Columbus and the beginnings of Spanish colonisation in the West Indies
4   The problem of the Aboriginees: a Spanish dilemma
5   The development of Spanish colonial administration and trade in the West Indies during the first half of the 16th century
6   The privateering challenge to Spain: War and trade in the West Indies during the later 16th century
7   The development of colonial society in the Spanish West Indies during the later 16th century
8   The overthrow of Spain's territorial monopoly in the West Indies
9   The proprietary regimes in the new European colonies in the West Indies
10   Dutch trade and the sugar revolution in the new European colonies in the West Indies
11   The African connection and the West Indies
12   Colonial society in the Spanish West Indies during the 17th century
13   England and France reassert their interest in the West Indies
14   The development of colonial society in the English and French colonies in the West Indies under royal control
15   The West Indies and the European struggle for pre-eminence, 1667–1689
16   Summary: The development of European empires in the West Indies to 1689

Vol. 2   The old regime in the West Indies to 1815

1   A new balance of power in the West Indies, 1689–1715
*2   The development of the plantations to 1750 (Part 1, pp. 7–70, *1970*)
3   Commercial activities and organisation in the West Indies during the 18th century
4   International rivalries among the European nations in the West Indies to the end of the Seven Years' War
*5   An era of West Indian prosperity 1750–1775 (Part 1, pp. 71–111, *1970*)
6   West Indian society in the 18th century (including political organisation)
*7   The West Indian slave laws of the 18th century (Part 2, pp. 7–53, *1970*)
8   Slave resistance in the West Indies to 1789
9   The free coloured in the West Indies to 1789
10   Creole culture in the West Indies during the 18th century
11   European opinion and the West Indian community in the 18th century

12   Colonial reform and crisis 1763–1789 (a Chapter covering events from the end of the Seven Years' War to the aftermath of the American Revolution in the West Indies and the emergence of humanitarian societies)
13   The French Revolution in the West Indies
14   War and trade in the West Indies during the Revolutionary and Napoleonic wars
15   The abolition of the British slave trade in the West Indies
16   Point counter point: the rise of Haiti and the rise of Cuba
17   Summary: The old regime in the West Indies to 1815

Vol. 3   Emancipation and the new free society in the West Indies

 *1   A new balance of power: the 19th century (Part 2, pp. 55–96, *1970*)
  2   An isolated independence: Haiti and Santo Domingo in the 19th century
  3   The struggle for suppression in the slave trade to the West Indies
  4   Amelioration and emancipation in the British West Indies
  5   Apprenticeship and problems of full emancipation in the British West Indies
  6   The West Indian sugar industry and British free trade
  7   Emancipation in the French, Danish and Dutch colonies in the West Indies
  8   The smallholder in the West Indies after emancipation
  9   Immigration in the West Indies in the 19th century
 10   Sugar, slavery and politics in the Spanish West Indies
 11   Emancipation and the revolutionary movement in Cuba
 12   Emancipation and political developments in the West Indian colonies during the second half of the 19th century
 13   The West Indies and the growth of American influence from the late 19th century to the present day
 14   Colonial government and the problems of the West Indies, from the late 19th century to the present day
 15   The labour movement in the West Indies to the present day
 16   Developments towards self-government and independence in the West Indies to the present day
 17   Movements towards unification and cooperation in the West Indies to the present day

Chapter 18 onwards to be considered.
* indicates Chapters already published.